Preface

Microsoft Azure Security Engineer AZ 500: Microsoft Azure Security Engineer is a meticulously structured guide designed to provide IT security professionals with the knowledge and skills required to secure cloud environments within the Microsoft Azure ecosystem. As organizations increasingly migrate to the cloud, securing Azure infrastructures, managing identity and access, implementing threat protection, and maintaining security operations have become paramount. This book is aligned with the objectives of the AZ-500 certification, covering key aspects such as network security, data protection, security governance, and compliance. Through a methodical approach, this guide ensures that readers develop a comprehensive understanding of Azure security technologies, including Azure Active Directory, Azure Firewall, Azure Security Center, and advanced security controls, preparing them for both certification success and practical application in enterprise environments.

Beyond exam preparation, Microsoft Azure Security Engineer AZ 500: Microsoft Azure Security Engineer serves as a valuable resource for security professionals aiming to enhance their expertise in cloud security best practices. Each chapter integrates real-world scenarios, hands-on exercises, and self-assessment tools to reinforce learning and facilitate knowledge retention. Additionally, online test papers and expert-led video tutorials complement the content, bridging the gap between theoretical knowledge and practical implementation. Whether you are an aspiring Azure Security Engineer or an experienced IT professional seeking to validate and expand your security capabilities, this book provides the structured guidance necessary to excel in securing Azure environments and mitigating evolving cybersecurity threats.

Table of Contents

Chapter 1: Practice Questions & Answers Part 1

QUESTION 1

You need to meet the identity and access requirements for Group1. What should you do?

A. Add a membership rule to Group1.

B. Delete Group1. Create a new group named Group1 that has a membership type of Office 365. Add users and devices to the group.

C. Modify the membership rule of Group1.

D. Change the membership type of Group1 to Assigne

E. Create two groups that have dynamic membership

F. Add the new groups to Group1.

Answer: B

QUESTION 2

You need to ensure that User2 can implement PIM. What should you do first?

A. Assign User2 the Global administrator role.

B. Configure authentication methods for contoso.com.

C. Configure the identity secure score for contoso.com.

D. Enable multi-factor authentication (MFA) for User2.

Answer: A

QUESTION 3

Note: This question is part of a series of questions that present the same scenario. Each question in the series contains a unique solution that might meet the stated goals. Some question sets might have more than one correct solution, while others might not have a correct solution.

After you answer a question in this section, you will NOT be able to return to it. As a result, these questions will not appear in the review screen. You have an Azure Subscription named Sub1.

You have an Azure Storage account named Sa1 in a resource group named RG1.

Users and applications access the blob service and the file service in Sa1 by using several shared access signatures (SASs) and stored access policies. You discover that unauthorized users accessed both the file service and the blob service.
You need to revoke all access to Sa1.
Solution: You create a new stored access policy. Does this meet the goal?

A. Yes
B. No
Answer: A

QUESTION 4
Note: This question is part of a series of questions that present the same scenario. Each question in the series contains a unique solution that might meet the stated goals. Some question sets might have more than one correct solution, while others might not have a correct solution.
After you answer a question in this section, you will NOT be able to return to it. As a result, these questions will not appear in the review screen. You have a hybrid configuration of Azure Active Directory (AzureAD). You have an Azure HDInsight cluster on a virtual network.
You plan to allow users to authenticate to the cluster by using their on-premises Active Directory credentials. You need to configure the environment to support the planned authentication.
Solution: You deploy the On-premises data gateway to the on-premises network. Does this meet the goal?

A. Yes
B. No
Answer: B

QUESTION 5
You have an Azure subscription.
You create an Azure web app named Contoso1812 that uses an S1 App service plan.
You create a DNS record for www.contoso.com that points to the IP address of Contoso1812.

You need to ensure that users can access Contoso1812 by using the https://www.contoso.com URL. Which two actions should you perform? Each correct answer

presents part of the solution.
NOTE: Each correct selection is worth one point.

A. Turn on the system-assigned managed identity for Contoso1812.
B. Add a hostname to Contoso1812.
C. Scale out the App Service plan of Contoso1812.
D. Add a deployment slot to Contoso1812.
E. Scale up the App Service plan of Contoso1812.
Answer: BE

QUESTION 6
You need to ensure that users can access VM0. The solution must meet the platform protection requirements. What should you do?
A. Move VM0 to Subnet1.
B. On Firewall, configure a network traffic filtering rule.
C. Assign RT1 to AzureFirewallSubnet.
D. On Firewall, configure a DNAT rule.
Answer: A

QUESTION 7
You are evaluating the security of the network communication between the virtual machines in Sub2. For each of the following statements, select Yes if the statement is true. Otherwise, select No. NOTE: Each correct selection is worth one point.

Statement	Yes/No
From VMI , you can successfully ping the public IP address of VM2	
From VMI , you can successfully ping the private IP address ofVM3.	
From VMI , you can successfully ping the public IP address of VM5.	

A. Mastered

B. Not Mastered

Answer: A

QUESTION 8

You have Azure Resource Manager templates that you use to deploy Azure virtual machines.

You need to disable unused Windows features automatically as instances of the virtual machines are provisioned. What should you use?

A. device compliance policies in Microsoft Intune

B. Azure Automation State Configuration

C. application security groups

D. Azure Advisor

Answer: B

QUESTION 9

You are configuring an Azure Kubernetes Service (AKS) cluster that will connect to an Azure Container Registry.

You need to use the auto-generated service principal to authenticate to the Azure Container Registry. What should you create?

A. an Azure Active Directory (Azure AD) group

B. an Azure Active Directory (Azure AD) role assignment

C. an Azure Active Directory (Azure AD) user

D. a secret in Azure Key Vault

Answer: B

QUESTION 10

You have Azure virtual machines that have Update Management enabled. The virtual machines are configured as shown in the following table.

Name	Operating system	Region	Resource group
VMI	Windows Server 2012	East US	RGI
VM2	Windows Server 2012 R2	West US	RGI
VM3	Windows Server 2016	West US	RG2
VM4	Ubuntu server 18.04 LTS	West US	RG2
VM5	Red Hat Ente rise Linux 7.4	East US	RGI
VM6	CentOS 7.5	East US	RGI

You schedule two update deployments named Updatel and Update2. Updatel updates VM3. Update2 updates VM6.

Which additional virtual machines can be updated by using Updatel and Update2? To answer, select the appropriate options in the answer area. NOTE: Each correct selection is worth one point.

Hot Area:

Updatel :	VM2 only
	VM4 only
	VMI and VM2 only
	VMI, VM2, VM4, VM5, andVM6
Update2:	VM5 only
	VMI and VM5 only
	VM4 and VM5 only
	VMI, VM2, and VM5 only
	VMI VM2 VM3 VM4 and VM5

A. Mastered

B. Not Mastered

Answer: A

QUESTION 11

You have an Azure subscription named Sub1.

You create a virtual network that contains one subnet. On the subnet, you provision the virtual machines shown in the following table.

Name	Network Interface	Application security group assignment	IP addresses
VM1	NIC1	AppGroup12	10.0.0.10
VM2	NIC2	AppGroup12	10.0.0.11
VM3	NIC3	AppGroup3	10.0.0.100
VM4	NIC4	AppGroup4	10.0.0.200

Currently, you have not provisioned any network security groups (NSGs). You need to implement network security to meet the following requirements: Allow traffic to VM4 from VM3 only. Allow traffic from the Internet to VM1 and VM2 only. Minimize the number of NSGs and network security rules.

How many NSGs and network security rules should you create? To answer, select the appropriate options in the answer area. NOTE: Each correct selection is worth one point.

Hot Area:

NSGs:

1
2
3
4

Network security rules:

1
2
3
4

A. Mastered

B. Not Mastered

Answer: A

QUESTION 12

You have two Azure virtual machines in the East US2 region as shown in the following table.

Name	Operating System	Type	Tier
VMI	Windows Server 2008 R2	A3	Basic
VM2	Ubuntu 16.04-DAILY-LTS	L4s	Standard

You deploy and configure an Azure Key vault.

You need to ensure that you can enable Azure Disk Encryption on VM1 and VM2.

What should you modify on each virtual machine? To answer, select the appropriate options in the answer area. NOTE: Each correct selection is worth one point.

Hot Area:

VM1

The operating system version
The tier
The type

VM2

The operating system version
The tier
The type

A. Mastered

B. Not Mastered

Answer: A

QUESTION 13

You need to ensure that you can meet the security operations requirements. What should you do first?

A. Turn on Auto Provisioning in Security Center.

B. Integrate Security Center and Microsoft Cloud App Security.

C. Upgrade the pricing tier of Security Center to Standard.

D. Modify the Security Center workspace configuration.

Answer: C

QUESTION 14

You have an Azure subscription named Sub1.

In Azure Security Center, you have a security playbook named Play1. Play1 is configured to send an email message to a user named User1. You need to modify Play1 to send email messages to a distribution group named Alerts.

What should you use to modify Play1?

A. Azure DevOps

B. Azure Application Insights

C. Azure Monitor

D. Azure Logic Apps Designer

Answer: D

QUESTION 15

You have an Azure subscription named Sub1 that contains an Azure Log Analytics workspace named LAW1.

You have 100 on-premises servers that run Windows Server 2012 R2 and Windows Server 2016. The servers connect to LAW1. LAW1 is configured to collect security-related performance counters from the connected servers.

You need to configure alerts based on the data collected by LAW1. The solution must meet the following requirements: Alert rules must support dimensions.

The time it takes to generate an alert must be minimized.

Alert notifications must be generated only once when the alert is generated and once when the alert is resolved. Which signal type should you use when you create the alert rules?

A. Log

B. Log (Saved Query)

C. Metric

D. Activity Log

Answer: C

QUESTION 16

You need to configure WebApp1 to meet the data and application requirements.

Which two actions should you perform? Each correct answer presents part of the solution. NOTE: Each correct selection is worth one point.

A. Upload a public certificate.

B. Turn on the HTTPS Only protocol setting.

C. Set the Minimum TLS Version protocol setting to 1.2.

D. Change the pricing tier of the App Service plan.

E. Turn on the Incoming client certificates protocol setting.

Answer: AC

QUESTION 17

Your company has an Azure subscription named Sub1 that is associated to an Azure Active Directory (Azure AD) tenant named contoso.com. The company develops an application named App1. App1 is registered in Azure AD.

You need to ensure that App1 can access secrets in Azure Key Vault on behalf of the application users. What should you configure?

A. an application permission without admin consent

B. a delegated permission without admin consent

C. a delegated permission that requires admin consent

D. an application permission that requires admin consent

Answer: B

QUESTION 18

Your company has an Azure subscription named Sub1 that is associated to an Azure Active Directory Azure (Azure AD) tenant named contoso.com.

The company develops a mobile application named App1. App1 uses the OAuth 2 implicit grant type to acquire Azure AD access tokens. You need to register App1 in Azure AD.

What information should you obtain from the developer to register the application?

A. a redirect URI

B. a reply URL

C. a key

D. an application ID

Answer: A

QUESTION 19

You have an Azure subscription that contains an Azure key vault named Vault1. In Vault1, you create a secret named Secret1.

An application developer registers an application in Azure Active Directory (Azure AD). You need to ensure that the application can use Secret1. What should you do?

A. In Azure AD, create a role.

B. In Azure Key Vault, create a key.

C. In Azure Key Vault, create an access policy.

D. In Azure AD, enable Azure AD Application Proxy.

Answer: A

QUESTION 20

You have a hybrid configuration of Azure Active Directory (Azure AD).

All users have computers that run Windows 10 and are hybrid Azure AD joined.

You have an Azure SQL database that is configured to support Azure AD authentication.

Database developers must connect to the SQL database by using Microsoft SQL Server Management Studio (SSMS) and authenticate by using their on-premises Active Directory account.

You need to tell the developers which authentication method to use to connect to the SQL database from SSMS. The solution must minimize authentication prompts.

Which authentication method should you instruct the developers to use?

A. SQL Login

B. Active Directory – Universal with MFA support

C. Active Directory – Integrated

D. Active Directory – Password

Answer: C

QUESTION 21

Your company uses Azure DevOps.

You need to recommend a method to validate whether the code meets the company's quality standards and code review standards. What should you recommend implementing in Azure DevOps?

A. branch folders

B. branch permissions

C. branch policies

D. branch locking

Answer: C

QUESTION 22

Your company plans to create separate subscriptions for each department. Each subscription will be associated to the same Azure Active Directory (Azure AD) tenant.

You need to configure each subscription to have the same role assignments. What should you use?

A. Azure Security Center

B. Azure Blueprints

C. Azure AD Privileged Identity Management (PIM)

D. Azure Policy

Answer: C

QUESTION 23

You have an Azure subscription.

You create an Azure web app named Contoso1812 that uses an S1 App service plan.

You create a DNS record for www.contoso.com that points to the IP address of Contoso1812.

You need to ensure that users can access Contoso1812 by using the https://www.contoso.com URL. Which two actions should you perform? Each correct answer presents part of the solution.

NOTE: Each correct selection is worth one point.

A. Turn on the system-assigned managed identity for Contoso1812.

B. Add a hostname to Contoso1812.

C. Scale out the App Service plan of Contoso1812.

D. Add a deployment slot to Contoso1812.

E. Scale up the App Service plan of Contoso1812.

Answer: BE

QUESTION 24

You need to ensure that users can access VM0. The solution must meet the platform protection requirements. What should you do?

A. Move VM0 to Subnet1.

B. On Firewall, configure a network traffic filtering rule.

C. Assign RT1 to AzureFirewallSubnet.

D. On Firewall, configure a DNAT rule.

Answer: A

QUESTION 25

You have an Azure subscription named Sub1. Sub1 contains a virtual network named VNet1 that contains one subnet named Subnet1. You create a service endpoint for Subnet1.

Subnet1 contains an Azure virtual machine named VM1 that runs Ubuntu Server 18.04.

You need to deploy Docker containers to VM1. The containers must be able to access Azure Storage resources and Azure SQL databases by using the service endpoint.

A. Create an application security group and a network security group (NSG).

B. Edit the docker-compose.yml file.

C. Install the container network interface (CNI) plug-in.

Answer: C

QUESTION 26

You have an Azure subscription. The subscription contains Azure virtual machines that run Windows Server 2016.

You need to implement a policy to ensure that each virtual machine has a custom antimalware virtual machine extension installed. How should you complete the policy? To answer, select the appropriate options in the answer area.

NOTE: Each correct selection is worth one point. Hot Area:

A. Mastered

B. Not Mastered

Answer: A

QUESTION 27

You are configuring an Azure Kubernetes Service (AKS) cluster that will connect to an Azure Container Registry.

You need to use the auto-generated service principal to authenticate to the Azure Container Registry. What should you create?

A. an Azure Active Directory (Azure AD) group

B. an Azure Active Directory (Azure AD) role assignment

C. an Azure Active Directory (Azure AD) user

D. a secret in Azure Key Vault

Answer: B

QUESTION 28

You have an Azure key vault.

You need to delegate administrative access to the key vault to meet the following requirements: Provide a user named Userl with the ability to set advanced access policies for the key vault. Provide a user named User2 with the ability to add and delete certificates in the key vault. Use the principle of least privilege.

What should you use to assign access to each user? To answer, select the appropriate options in the answer area. NOTE: Each correct selection is worth one point.

A. Mastered

B. Not Mastered

Answer: A

QUESTION 29

You have an Azure subscription named Sub1 that is associated to an Azure Active Directory (Azure AD) tenant named contoso.com.

You are assigned the Global administrator role for the tenant. You are responsible for managing Azure Security Center settings. You need to create a custom sensitivity label.

What should you do first?

A. Create a custom sensitive information type.

B. Elevate access for global administrators in Azure AD.

C. Upgrade the pricing tier of the Security Center to Standard.

D. Enable integration with Microsoft Cloud App Security.

Answer: A

QUESTION 30

You suspect that users are attempting to sign in to resources to which they have no access.

You need to create an Azure Log Analytics query to identify failed user sign-in attempts from the last three days. The results must only show users who had more than five failed sign-in attempts.

How should you configure the query? To answer, select the appropriate options in the answer area.

NOTE: Each correct selection is worth one point.

A. Mastered

B. Not Mastered

Answer: A

QUESTION 31

You have an Azure subscription that contains 100 virtual machines. Azure Diagnostics is enabled on all the virtual machines. You are planning the monitoring of Azure services in the subscription.

You need to retrieve the following details:

Identify the user who deleted a virtual machine three weeks ago.

Query the security events of a virtual machine that runs Windows Server 2016.

What should you use in Azure Monitor? To answer, drag the appropriate configuration settings to the correct details. Each configuration setting may be used once, more than once, or not at all. You may need to drag the split bar between panes or scroll to view content.
NOTE: Each correct selection is worth one point. Select and Place:

A. Mastered
B. Not Mastered
Answer: A

QUESTION 32
You need to create Role1 to meet the platform protection requirements.
How should you complete the role definition of Role1? To answer, select the appropriate options in the answer area. NOTE: Each correct selection is worth one point.
A. Mastered
B. Not Mastered
Answer: A

QUESTION 33
Your company has an Azure subscription named Sub1 that is associated to an Azure Active Directory (Azure AD) tenant named contoso.com. The company develops an application named App1. App1 is registered in Azure AD.
You need to ensure that App1 can access secrets in Azure Key Vault on behalf of the application users. What should you configure?

A. an application permission without admin consent
B. a delegated permission without admin consent
C. a delegated permission that requires admin consent
D. an application permission that requires admin consent
Answer: B

QUESTION 34

You have an Azure subscription named Sub1 that is associated to an Azure Active Directory (Azure AD) tenant named contoso.com. You plan to implement an application that will consist of the resources shown in the following table.

Users will authenticate by using their Azure AD user account and access the Cosmos DB account by using resource tokens. You need to identify which tasks will be implemented in CosmosDB1 and WebApp1.

Which task should you identify for each resource? To answer, select the appropriate options in the answer area. NOTE: Each correct selection is worth one point.

A. Mastered

B. Not Mastered

Answer: A

QUESTION 35

You have an Azure subscription named Sub1 that contains an Azure Storage account named Contosostorage1 and an Azure key vault named Contosokeyvault1. You plan to create an Azure Automation runbook that will rotate the keys of Contosostorage1 and store them in Contosokeyvault1.

You need to implement prerequisites to ensure that you can implement the runbook.

Which three actions should you perform in sequence? To answer, move the appropriate actions from the list of actions to the answer area and arrange them in the correct order.

Select and Place:

A. Mastered

B. Not Mastered

Answer: A

QUESTION 36

You need to meet the identity and access requirements for Group1. What should you do?

A. Add a membership rule to Group1.

B. Delete Group1. Create a new group named Group1 that has a membership type of Office 365. Add users and devices to the group.

C. Modify the membership rule of Group1.

D. Change the membership type of Group1 to Assigne

E. Create two groups that have dynamic membership

F. Add the new groups to Group1.

Answer: B

QUESTION 37

Note: This question is part of a series of questions that present the same scenario. Each question in the series contains a unique solution that might meet the stated goals. Some question sets might have more than one correct solution, while others might not have a correct solution.

After you answer a question in this section, you will NOT be able to return to it. As a result, these questions will not appear in the review screen. You have a hybrid configuration of Azure Active Directory (AzureAD). You have an Azure HDInsight cluster on a virtual network.

You plan to allow users to authenticate to the cluster by using their on-premises Active Directory credentials. You need to configure the environment to support the planned authentication.

Solution: You deploy the On-premises data gateway to the on-premises network. Does this meet the goal?

A. Yes

B. No

Answer: B

QUESTION 38

Your network contains an on-premises Active Directory domain named corp.contoso.com.

You have an Azure subscription named Sub1 that is associated to an Azure Active Directory (Azure AD) tenant named contoso.com. You sync all on-premises identities to Azure AD.

You need to prevent users who have a givenName attribute that starts with TEST from being synced to Azure AD. The solution must minimize administrative effort. What should you use?

A. Synchronization Rules Editor

B. Web Service Configuration Tool

C. the Azure AD Connect wizard

D. Active Directory Users and Computers

Answer: A

QUESTION 39

You are implementing conditional access policies.

You must evaluate the existing Azure Active Directory (Azure AD) risk events and risk levels to configure and implement the policies. You need to identify the risk level of the following risk events:

Users with leaked credentials Impossible travel to atypical locations Sign ins from IP addresses with suspicious activity

Which level should you identify for each risk event? To answer, drag the appropriate levels to the correct risk events. Each level may be used once, more than once, or not at all. You may need to drag the split bar between panes or scroll to view content.

A. Mastered

B. Not Mastered

Answer: A

QUESTION 40

You need to configure an access review. The review will be assigned to a new collection of reviews and reviewed by resource owners.

Which three actions should you perform in sequence? To answer, move the appropriate actions from the list of actions to the answer area and arrange them in the correct order.

A. Mastered

B. Not Mastered

Answer: A

QUESTION 41

You create an Azure subscription.

You need to ensure that you can use Azure Active Directory (Azure AD) Privileged Identity Management (PIM) to secure Azure AD roles.

Which three actions should you perform in sequence? To answer, move the appropriate actions from the list of actions to the answer area and arrange them in the correct order.

A. Mastered

B. Not Mastered

Answer: A

QUESTION 42

You have an Azure subscription.

You create an Azure web app named Contoso1812 that uses an S1 App service plan.

You create a DNS record for www.contoso.com that points to the IP address of Contoso1812.

You need to ensure that users can access Contoso1812 by using the https://www.contoso.com URL. Which two actions should you perform? Each correct answer presents part of the solution.

NOTE: Each correct selection is worth one point.

A. Turn on the system-assigned managed identity for Contoso1812.

B. Add a hostname to Contoso1812.

C. Scale out the App Service plan of Contoso1812.

D. Add a deployment slot to Contoso1812.

E. Scale up the App Service plan of Contoso1812.

Answer: BE

QUESTION 43

You need to ensure that users can access VM0. The solution must meet the platform protection requirements. What should you do?

A. Move VM0 to Subnet1.

B. On Firewall, configure a network traffic filtering rule.

C. Assign RT1 to AzureFirewallSubnet.

D. On Firewall, configure a DNAT rule.

Answer: A

QUESTION 44

You have an Azure subscription named Sub1. Sub1 contains a virtual network named VNet1 that contains one subnet named Subnet1.

You create a service endpoint for Subnet1.

Subnet1 contains an Azure virtual machine named VM1 that runs Ubuntu Server 18.04.

You need to deploy Docker containers to VM1. The containers must be able to access Azure Storage resources and Azure SQL databases by using the service endpoint.

A. Create an application security group and a network security group (NSG).

B. Edit the docker-compose.yml file.

C. Install the container network interface (CNI) plug-in.

Answer: C

QUESTION 45

You have an Azure key vault.

You need to delegate administrative access to the key vault to meet the following requirements:

Provide a user named User1 with the ability to set advanced access policies for the key vault.

Provide a user named User2 with the ability to add and delete certificates in the key vault. Use the principle of least privilege.

What should you use to assign access to each user? To answer, select the appropriate options in the answer area. NOTE: Each correct selection is worth one point.

A. Mastered

B. Not Mastered

Answer: A

QUESTION 46

You have an Azure virtual machines shown in the following table.

You create an Azure Log Analytics workspace named Analytics1 in RG1 in the East US region. Which virtual machines can be enrolled in Analytics1?

A. VM1 only

B. VM1, VM2, and VM3 only

C. VM1, VM2, VM3, and VM4

D. VM1 and VM4 only

Answer: A

QUESTION 47

You are testing an Azure Kubernetes Service (AKS) cluster. The cluster is configured as shown in the exhibit. (Click the Exhibit tab.)

You plan to deploy the cluster to production. You disable HTTP application routing.

You need to implement application routing that will provide reverse proxy and TLS termination for AKS services by using a single IP address. What should you do?

A. Create an AKS Ingress controller.

B. Install the container network interface (CNI) plug-in.

C. Create an Azure Standard Load Balancer.

D. Create an Azure Basic Load Balancer.

Answer: A

QUESTION 48

You assign User8 the Owner role for RG4, RG5, and RG6.

In which resource groups can User8 create virtual networks and NSGs? To answer, select the appropriate options in the answer area. NOTE: Each correct selection is worth one point.

A. Mastered

B. Not Mastered

Answer: A

QUESTION 49

You have an Azure subscription named Sub1 that is associated to an Azure Active Directory (Azure AD) tenant named contoso.com.

You are assigned the Global administrator role for the tenant. You are responsible for managing Azure Security Center settings. You need to create a custom sensitivity label.

What should you do first?

A. Create a custom sensitive information type.

B. Elevate access for global administrators in Azure AD.

C. Upgrade the pricing tier of the Security Center to Standard.

D. Enable integration with Microsoft Cloud App Security.

Answer: A

QUESTION 43

You create a new Azure subscription.

You need to ensure that you can create custom alert rules in Azure Security Center. Which two actions should you perform? Each correct answer presents part of the solution. NOTE: Each correct selection is worth one point.

A. Onboard Azure Active Directory (Azure AD) Identity Protection.

B. Create an Azure Storage account.

C. Implement Azure Advisor recommendations.

D. Create an Azure Log Analytics workspace.

E. Upgrade the pricing tier of Security Center to Standard.

Answer: BD

QUESTION 50

You need to create Role1 to meet the platform protection requirements.

How should you complete the role definition of Role1? To answer, select the appropriate options in the answer area. NOTE: Each correct selection is worth one point.

A. Mastered

B. Not Mastered

Answer: A

QUESTION 51

You need to configure SQLDB1 to meet the data and application requirements.

Which three actions should you recommend be performed in sequence? To answer, move the appropriate actions from the list of actions to the answer area and arrange them in the correct order.

Select and Place:

A. Mastered

B. Not Mastered

Answer: A

QUESTION 52

Your company has an Azure subscription named Sub1 that is associated to an Azure Active Directory Azure (Azure AD) tenant named contoso.com.

The company develops a mobile application named App1. App1 uses the OAuth 2 implicit grant type to acquire Azure AD access tokens. You need to register App1 in Azure AD.

What information should you obtain from the developer to register the application?

A. a redirect URI

B. a reply URL

C. a key

D. an application ID

Answer: A

QUESTION 53

From the Azure portal, you are configuring an Azure policy.

You plan to assign policies that use the DeployIfNotExist, AuditIfNotExist, Append, and Deny effects. Which effect requires a managed identity for the assignment?

A. AuditIfNotExist

B. Append

C. DeployIfNotExist

D. Deny

Answer: C

QUESTION 54

You have an Azure subscription that contains an Azure key vault named Vault1. In Vault1, you create a secret named Secret1.

An application developer registers an application in Azure Active Directory (Azure AD). You need to ensure that the application can use Secret1. What should you do?

A. In Azure AD, create a role.

B. In Azure Key Vault, create a key.

C. In Azure Key Vault, create an access policy.

D. In Azure AD, enable Azure AD Application Proxy.

Answer: A

QUESTION 55

You have an Azure SQL database.

You implement Always Encrypted.

You need to ensure that application developers can retrieve and decrypt data in the database.

Which two pieces of information should you provide to the developers? Each correct answer presents part of the solution. NOTE: Each correct selection is worth one point.

A. a stored access policy

B. a shared access signature (SAS)

C. the column encryption key

D. user credentials

E. the column master key

Answer: CE

QUESTION 56

You need to meet the identity and access requirements for Group1. What should you do?

A. Add a membership rule to Group1.

B. Delete Group1. Create a new group named Group1 that has a membership type of Office 365. Add users and devices to the group.

C. Modify the membership rule of Group1.

D. Change the membership type of Group1 to Assigne

E. Create two groups that have dynamic membership

F. Add the new groups to Group1.

Answer: B

QUESTION 57

Note: This question is part of a series of questions that present the same scenario. Each question in the series contains a unique solution that might meet the stated goals. Some question sets might have more than one correct solution, while others might not have a correct solution.

After you answer a question in this section, you will NOT be able to return to it. As a result, these questions will not appear in the review screen. You have a hybrid configuration of Azure Active Directory (AzureAD). You have an Azure HDInsight cluster on a virtual network.

You plan to allow users to authenticate to the cluster by using their on-premises Active Directory credentials. You need to configure the environment to support the planned authentication.

Solution: You deploy the On-premises data gateway to the on-premises network. Does this meet the goal?

A. Yes

B. No

Answer: B

QUESTION 58

Your network contains an on-premises Active Directory domain named corp.contoso.com.

You have an Azure subscription named Sub1 that is associated to an Azure Active Directory (Azure AD) tenant named contoso.com. You sync all on-premises identities to Azure AD.

You need to prevent users who have a givenName attribute that starts with TEST from being synced to Azure AD. The solution must minimize administrative effort. What should you use?

A. Synchronization Rules Editor

B. Web Service Configuration Tool

C. the Azure AD Connect wizard

D. Active Directory Users and Computers

Answer: A

QUESTION 59

You are implementing conditional access policies.

You must evaluate the existing Azure Active Directory (Azure AD) risk events and risk levels to configure and implement the policies. You need to identify the risk level of the following risk events:

Users with leaked credentials Impossible travel to atypical locations Sign ins from IP addresses with suspicious activity

Which level should you identify for each risk event? To answer, drag the appropriate levels to the correct risk events. Each level may be used once, more than once, or not at all. You may need to drag the split bar between panes or scroll to view content.

A. Mastered

B. Not Mastered

Answer: A

Chapter 2: Practice Questions & Answers Part 2

QUESTION 60

You need to configure an access review. The review will be assigned to a new collection of reviews and reviewed by resource owners.

Which three actions should you perform in sequence? To answer, move the appropriate actions from the list of actions to the answer area and arrange them in the correct order.

A. Mastered

B. Not Mastered

Answer: A

QUESTION 61

You have an Azure subscription.

You create an Azure web app named Contoso1812 that uses an S1 App service plan.

You create a DNS record for www.contoso.com that points to the IP address of Contoso1812.

You need to ensure that users can access Contoso1812 by using the https://www.contoso.com URL. Which two actions should you perform? Each correct answer presents part of the solution.

NOTE: Each correct selection is worth one point.

A. Turn on the system-assigned managed identity for Contoso1812.

B. Add a hostname to Contoso1812.

C. Scale out the App Service plan of Contoso1812.

D. Add a deployment slot to Contoso1812.

E. Scale up the App Service plan of Contoso1812.

Answer: BE

QUESTION 62

You need to ensure that users can access VM0. The solution must meet the platform protection requirements. What should you do?

A. Move VM0 to Subnet1.

B. On Firewall, configure a network traffic filtering rule.

C. Assign RT1 to AzureFirewallSubnet.

D. On Firewall, configure a DNAT rule.

Answer: A

QUESTION 63

You have an Azure subscription named Sub1. Sub1 contains a virtual network named VNet1 that contains one subnet named Subnet1.

You create a service endpoint for Subnet1.

Subnet1 contains an Azure virtual machine named VM1 that runs Ubuntu Server 18.04.

You need to deploy Docker containers to VM1. The containers must be able to access Azure Storage resources and Azure SQL databases by using the service endpoint.

A. Create an application security group and a network security group (NSG).

B. Edit the docker-compose.yml file.

C. Install the container network interface (CNI) plug-in.

Answer: C

QUESTION 64

You have an Azure virtual machines shown in the following table.

You create an Azure Log Analytics workspace named Analytics1 in RG1 in the East US region.

Which virtual machines can be enrolled in Analytics1?

A. VM1 only

B. VM1, VM2, and VM3 only

C. VM1, VM2, VM3, and VM4

D. VM1 and VM4 only

Answer: A

QUESTION 65

You are testing an Azure Kubernetes Service (AKS) cluster. The cluster is configured as shown in the exhibit. (Click the Exhibit tab.)

You plan to deploy the cluster to production. You disable HTTP application routing.

You need to implement application routing that will provide reverse proxy and TLS termination for AKS services by using a single IP address. What should you do?

A. Create an AKS Ingress controller.

B. Install the container network interface (CNI) plug-in.

C. Create an Azure Standard Load Balancer.

D. Create an Azure Basic Load Balancer.

Answer: A

QUESTION 66

You have an Azure subscription named Sub1 that is associated to an Azure Active Directory (Azure AD) tenant named contoso.com.

You are assigned the Global administrator role for the tenant. You are responsible for managing Azure Security Center settings. You need to create a custom sensitivity label.

What should you do first?

A. Create a custom sensitive information type.

B. Elevate access for global administrators in Azure AD.

C. Upgrade the pricing tier of the Security Center to Standard.

D. Enable integration with Microsoft Cloud App Security.

Answer: A

QUESTION 67

You have an Azure subscription named Sub1.

In Azure Security Center, you have a security playbook named Play1. Play1 is configured to send an email message to a user named User1. You need to modify

Play1 to send email messages to a distribution group named Alerts. What should you use to modify Play1?

A. Azure DevOps

B. Azure Application Insights

C. Azure Monitor

D. Azure Logic Apps Designer

Answer: D

QUESTION 68

You create a new Azure subscription.

You need to ensure that you can create custom alert rules in Azure Security Center. Which two actions should you perform? Each correct answer presents part of the solution. NOTE: Each correct selection is worth one point.

A. Onboard Azure Active Directory (Azure AD) Identity Protection.

B. Create an Azure Storage account.

C. Implement Azure Advisor recommendations.

D. Create an Azure Log Analytics workspace.

E. Upgrade the pricing tier of Security Center to Standard.

Answer: BD

QUESTION 69

Your company has an Azure subscription named Sub1 that is associated to an Azure Active Directory Azure (Azure AD) tenant named contoso.com.

The company develops a mobile application named App1. App1 uses the OAuth 2 implicit grant type to acquire Azure AD access tokens. You need to register App1 in Azure AD.

What information should you obtain from the developer to register the application?

A. a redirect URI

B. a reply URL

C. a key

D. an application ID

Answer: A

QUESTION 70

From the Azure portal, you are configuring an Azure policy.

You plan to assign policies that use the DeployIfNotExist, AuditIfNotExist, Append, and Deny effects. Which effect requires a managed identity for the assignment?

A. AuditIfNotExist

B. Append

C. DeployIfNotExist

D. Deny

Answer: C

QUESTION 71

You have an Azure subscription named Sub1 that is associated to an Azure Active Directory (Azure AD) tenant named contoso.com. You plan to implement an application that will consist of the resources shown in the following table.

Users will authenticate by using their Azure AD user account and access the Cosmos DB account by using resource tokens. You need to identify which tasks will be implemented in CosmosDB1 and WebApp1.

Which task should you identify for each resource? To answer, select the appropriate options in the answer area. NOTE: Each correct selection is worth one point.

A. Mastered

B. Not Mastered

Answer: A

QUESTION 72

You have an Azure subscription that contains an Azure key vault named Vault1. In Vault1, you create a secret named Secret1.

An application developer registers an application in Azure Active Directory (Azure AD). You need to ensure that the application can use Secret1. What should you do?

A. In Azure AD, create a role.

B. In Azure Key Vault, create a key.

C. In Azure Key Vault, create an access policy.

D. In Azure AD, enable Azure AD Application Proxy.

Answer: A

QUESTION 73

You have an Azure SQL database.

You implement Always Encrypted.

You need to ensure that application developers can retrieve and decrypt data in the database.

Which two pieces of information should you provide to the developers? Each correct answer presents part of the solution. NOTE: Each correct selection is worth one point.

A. a stored access policy

B. a shared access signature (SAS)

C. the column encryption key

D. user credentials

E. the column master key

Answer: CE

QUESTION 74

You need to ensure that User2 can implement PIM. What should you do first?

A. Assign User2 the Global administrator role.

B. Configure authentication methods for contoso.com.

C. Configure the identity secure score for contoso.com.

D. Enable multi-factor authentication (MFA) for User2.

Answer: A

QUESTION 75

Note: This question is part of a series of questions that present the same scenario. Each question in the series contains a unique solution that might meet the stated goals. Some question sets might have more than one correct solution, while others might not have a correct solution.

After you answer a question in this section, you will NOT be able to return to it. As a result, these questions will not appear in the review screen. You have a hybrid configuration of Azure Active Directory (AzureAD). You have an Azure HDInsight cluster on a virtual network.

You plan to allow users to authenticate to the cluster by using their on-premises Active Directory credentials. You need to configure the environment to support the planned authentication.
Solution: You deploy the On-premises data gateway to the on-premises network. Does this meet the goal?

A. Yes
B. No
Answer: B

QUESTION 76
You have an Azure Active Directory (Azure AD) tenant named contoso.com. The tenant contains the users shown in the following table.
You configure an access review named Review1 as shown in the following exhibit.

Use the drop-down menus to select the answer choice that completes each statement based on the information presented in the graphic. NOTE: Each correct selection is worth one point.
A. Mastered
B. Not Mastered
Answer: A

QUESTION 77
Your company plans to create separate subscriptions for each department. Each subscription will be associated to the same Azure Active Directory (Azure AD) tenant.
You need to configure each subscription to have the same role assignments. What should you use?

A. Azure Security Center
B. Azure Blueprints
C. Azure AD Privileged Identity Management (PIM)
D. Azure Policy
Answer: C

QUESTION 78

You have Azure Resource Manager templates that you use to deploy Azure virtual machines. You need to disable unused Windows features automatically as instances of the virtual machines are provisioned. What should you use?

A. device compliance policies in Microsoft Intune

B. Azure Automation State Configuration

C. application security groups

D. Azure Advisor

Answer: B

QUESTION 79

You have an Azure subscription that contains the virtual networks shown in the following table.

The Azure virtual machines on SpokeVNetSubnet0 can communicate with the computers on the on-premises network. You plan to deploy an Azure firewall to HubVNet.

You create the following two routing tables:

RT1: Includes a user-defined route that points to the private IP address of the Azure firewall as a next hop address RT2: Disables BGP route propagation and defines the private IP address of the Azure firewall as the default gateway

You need to ensure that traffic between SpokeVNetSubnet0 and the on-premises network flows through the Azure firewall.

To which subnet should you associate each route table? To answer, drag the appropriate subnets to the correct route tables. Each subnet may be used once, more than once, or not at all. You may need to drag the split bar between panes or scroll to view content.

A. Mastered

B. Not Mastered

Answer: A

QUESTION 80

You are testing an Azure Kubernetes Service (AKS) cluster. The cluster is configured as shown in the exhibit. (Click the Exhibit tab.)
You plan to deploy the cluster to production. You disable HTTP application routing.
You need to implement application routing that will provide reverse proxy and TLS termination for AKS services by using a single IP address. What should you do?

A. Create an AKS Ingress controller.
B. Install the container network interface (CNI) plug-in.
C. Create an Azure Standard Load Balancer.
D. Create an Azure Basic Load Balancer.
Answer: A

QUESTION 82
You need to ensure that you can meet the security operations requirements. What should you do first?

A. Turn on Auto Provisioning in Security Center.
B. Integrate Security Center and Microsoft Cloud App Security.
C. Upgrade the pricing tier of Security Center to Standard.
D. Modify the Security Center workspace configuration.
Answer: C

QUESTION 83
You have an Azure subscription named Sub1 that is associated to an Azure Active Directory (Azure AD) tenant named contoso.com.
You are assigned the Global administrator role for the tenant. You are responsible for managing Azure Security Center settings. You need to create a custom sensitivity label.
What should you do first?

A. Create a custom sensitive information type.
B. Elevate access for global administrators in Azure AD.

C. Upgrade the pricing tier of the Security Center to Standard.

D. Enable integration with Microsoft Cloud App Security.

Answer: A

QUESTION 84

You need to configure WebApp1 to meet the data and application requirements.

Which two actions should you perform? Each correct answer presents part of the solution. NOTE: Each correct selection is worth one point.

A. Upload a public certificate.

B. Turn on the HTTPS Only protocol setting.

C. Set the Minimum TLS Version protocol setting to 1.2.

D. Change the pricing tier of the App Service plan.

E. Turn on the Incoming client certificates protocol setting.

Answer: AC

QUESTION 85

From the Azure portal, you are configuring an Azure policy.

You plan to assign policies that use the DeployIfNotExist, AuditIfNotExist, Append, and Deny effects. Which effect requires a managed identity for the assignment?

A. AuditIfNotExist

B. Append

C. DeployIfNotExist

D. Deny

Answer: C

QUESTION 86

You need to configure an access review. The review will be assigned to a new collection of reviews and reviewed by resource owners.

Which three actions should you perform in sequence? To answer, move the appropriate actions from the list of actions to the answer area and arrange them in the correct order.

A. Mastered

B. Not Mastered

Answer: A

QUESTION 87

Your company plans to create separate subscriptions for each department. Each subscription will be associated to the same Azure Active Directory (Azure AD) tenant.

You need to configure each subscription to have the same role assignments. What should you use?

A. Azure Security Center

B. Azure Blueprints

C. Azure AD Privileged Identity Management (PIM)

D. Azure Policy

Answer: C

QUESTION 88

You have Azure Resource Manager templates that you use to deploy Azure virtual machines.

You need to disable unused Windows features automatically as instances of the virtual machines are provisioned. What should you use?

A. device compliance policies in Microsoft Intune

B. Azure Automation State Configuration

C. application security groups

D. Azure Advisor

Answer: B

QUESTION 89

You are configuring an Azure Kubernetes Service (AKS) cluster that will connect to an Azure Container Registry.

You need to use the auto-generated service principal to authenticate to the Azure Container Registry. What should you create?

A. an Azure Active Directory (Azure AD) group

B. an Azure Active Directory (Azure AD) role assignment

C. an Azure Active Directory (Azure AD) user

D. a secret in Azure Key Vault

Answer: B

QUESTION 90

You have an Azure subscription that contains the virtual machines shown in the following table.

You create the Azure policies shown in the following table.

You create the resource locks shown in the following table.

For each of the following statements, select Yes if the statement is true. Otherwise, select No.

NOTE: Each correct selection is worth one point.

A. Mastered

B. Not Mastered

Answer: A

QUESTION 91

You need to ensure that you can meet the security operations requirements. What should you do first?

A. Turn on Auto Provisioning in Security Center.

B. Integrate Security Center and Microsoft Cloud App Security.

C. Upgrade the pricing tier of Security Center to Standard.

D. Modify the Security Center workspace configuration.

Answer: C

QUESTION 92

You plan to use Azure Log Analytics to collect logs from 200 servers that run Windows Server 2016.

You need to automate the deployment of the Microsoft Monitoring Agent to all the servers by using an Azure Resource Manager template. How should you complete the template?

A. Mastered

B. Not Mastered

Answer: A Explanation:

QUESTION 93

You create a new Azure subscription.

You need to ensure that you can create custom alert rules in Azure Security Center. Which two actions should you perform? Each correct answer presents part of the solution. NOTE: Each correct selection is worth one point.

A. Onboard Azure Active Directory (Azure AD) Identity Protection.

B. Create an Azure Storage account.

C. Implement Azure Advisor recommendations.

D. Create an Azure Log Analytics workspace.

E. Upgrade the pricing tier of Security Center to Standard.

Answer: BD

QUESTION 94

Your company has an Azure subscription named Sub1 that is associated to an Azure Active Directory Azure (Azure AD) tenant named contoso.com.

The company develops a mobile application named App1. App1 uses the OAuth 2 implicit grant type to acquire Azure AD access tokens. You need to register App1 in Azure AD.

What information should you obtain from the developer to register the application?

A. a redirect URI

B. a reply URL

C. a key

D. an application ID

Answer: A

QUESTION 95

You have an Azure subscription named Sub1 that is associated to an Azure Active Directory (Azure AD) tenant named contoso.com. You plan to implement an application that will consist of the resources shown in the following table.

Users will authenticate by using their Azure AD user account and access the Cosmos DB account by using resource tokens. You need to identify which tasks will be implemented in CosmosDB1 and WebApp1.

Which task should you identify for each resource?

Answer: A

QUESTION 96

You have an Azure subscription that contains an Azure key vault named Vault1. In Vault1, you create a secret named Secret1.

An application developer registers an application in Azure Active Directory (Azure AD). You need to ensure that the application can use Secret1. What should you do?

A. In Azure AD, create a role.

B. In Azure Key Vault, create a key.

C. In Azure Key Vault, create an access policy.

D. In Azure AD, enable Azure AD Application Proxy.

Answer: A

QUESTION 97

You need to meet the identity and access requirements for Group1. What should you do?

A. Add a membership rule to Group1.

B. Delete Group1. Create a new group named Group1 that has a membership type of Office 365. Add users and devices to the group.

C. Modify the membership rule of Group1.

D. Change the membership type of Group1 to Assign

E. Create two groups that have dynamic membership

F. Add the new groups to Group1.

Answer: B

QUESTION 98

Note: This question is part of a series of questions that present the same scenario. Each question in the series contains a unique solution that might meet the stated goals. Some question sets might have more than one correct solution, while others might not have a correct solution.

After you answer a question in this section, you will NOT be able to return to it. As a result, these questions will not appear in the review screen. You have a hybrid configuration of Azure Active Directory (AzureAD). You have an Azure HDInsight cluster on a virtual network.

You plan to allow users to authenticate to the cluster by using their on-premises Active Directory credentials. You need to configure the environment to support the planned authentication.

Solution: You deploy the On-premises data gateway to the on-premises network. Does this meet the goal?

A. Yes

B. No

Answer: B

QUESTION 99

Your network contains an on-premises Active Directory domain named corp.contoso.com.

You have an Azure subscription named Sub1 that is associated to an Azure Active Directory (Azure AD) tenant named contoso.com. You sync all on-premises identities to Azure AD.

You need to prevent users who have a givenName attribute that starts with TEST from being synced to Azure AD. The solution must minimize administrative effort. What should you use?

A. Synchronization Rules Editor

B. Web Service Configuration Tool

C. the Azure AD Connect wizard

D. Active Directory Users and Computers

Answer: A

QUESTION 100

You are implementing conditional access policies.

You must evaluate the existing Azure Active Directory (Azure AD) risk events and risk levels to configure and implement the policies. You need to identify the risk level of the following risk events:

Users with leaked credentials Impossible travel to atypical locations Sign ins from IP addresses with suspicious activity

Which level should you identify for each risk event? To answer, drag the appropriate levels to the correct risk events. Each level may be used once, more than once, or not at all. You may need to drag the split bar between panes or scroll to view content.

A. Mastered

B. Not Mastered

Answer: A

QUESTION 101

You need to configure an access review. The review will be assigned to a new collection of reviews and reviewed by resource owners.

Which three actions should you perform in sequence?

A. Mastered

B. Not Mastered

Answer: A

QUESTION 102

You create an Azure subscription.

You need to ensure that you can use Azure Active Directory (Azure AD) Privileged Identity Management (PIM) to secure Azure AD roles.

Which three actions should you perform in sequence? To answer, move the appropriate actions from the list of actions to the answer area and arrange them in the correct order.

Select and Place:

A. Mastered

B. Not Mastered

Answer: A

QUESTION 103

You have an Azure subscription.

You create an Azure web app named Contoso1812 that uses an S1 App service plan.

You create a DNS record for www.contoso.com that points to the IP address of Contoso1812.

You need to ensure that users can access Contoso1812 by using the https://www.contoso.com URL. Which two actions should you perform? Each correct answer presents part of the solution.

NOTE: Each correct selection is worth one point.

A. Turn on the system-assigned managed identity for Contoso1812.

B. Add a hostname to Contoso1812.

C. Scale out the App Service plan of Contoso1812.

D. Add a deployment slot to Contoso1812.

E. Scale up the App Service plan of Contoso1812.

Answer: BE

QUESTION 104

You need to ensure that users can access VM0. The solution must meet the platform protection requirements. What should you do?

A. Move VM0 to Subnet1.

B. On Firewall, configure a network traffic filtering rule.

C. Assign RT1 to AzureFirewallSubnet.

D. On Firewall, configure a DNAT rule.

Answer: A

QUESTION 105

You have an Azure subscription named Sub1. Sub1 contains a virtual network named VNet1 that contains one subnet named Subnet1.

You create a service endpoint for Subnet1.

Subnet1 contains an Azure virtual machine named VM1 that runs Ubuntu Server 18.04.

You need to deploy Docker containers to VM1. The containers must be able to access Azure Storage resources and Azure SQL databases by using the service endpoint.

A. Create an application security group and a network security group (NSG).

B. Edit the docker-compose.yml file.

C. Install the container network interface (CNI) plug-in.

Answer: C

QUESTION 106

You have an Azure subscription. The subscription contains Azure virtual machines that run Windows Server 2016.

You need to implement a policy to ensure that each virtual machine has a custom antimalware virtual machine extension installed. How should you complete the policy?

A. Mastered

B. Not Mastered

Answer: A

QUESTION 107

You have an Azure virtual machines shown in the following table.

You create an Azure Log Analytics workspace named Analytics1 in RG1 in the East US region. Which virtual machines can be enrolled in Analytics1?

A. VM1 only

B. VM1, VM2, and VM3 only

C. VM1, VM2, VM3, and VM4

D. VM1 and VM4 only

Answer: A

QUESTION 108

You are testing an Azure Kubernetes Service (AKS) cluster. The cluster is configured as shown in the exhibit. (Click the Exhibit tab.)

You plan to deploy the cluster to production. You disable HTTP application routing.

You need to implement application routing that will provide reverse proxy and TLS termination for AKS services by using a single IP address. What should you do?

A. Create an AKS Ingress controller.

B. Install the container network interface (CNI) plug-in.

C. Create an Azure Standard Load Balancer.

D. Create an Azure Basic Load Balancer.

Answer: A

QUESTION 109

You assign User8 the Owner role for RG4, RG5, and RG6.

In which resource groups can User8 create virtual networks and NSGs?

A. Mastered

B. Not Mastered

Answer: A

QUESTION 110

You have an Azure subscription named Sub1 that is associated to an Azure Active Directory (Azure AD) tenant named contoso.com.

You are assigned the Global administrator role for the tenant. You are responsible for managing Azure Security Center settings. You need to create a custom sensitivity label.

What should you do first?

A. Create a custom sensitive information type.

B. Elevate access for global administrators in Azure AD.

C. Upgrade the pricing tier of the Security Center to Standard.

D. Enable integration with Microsoft Cloud App Security.

Answer: A

QUESTION 111

You have an Azure subscription named Sub1.

In Azure Security Center, you have a security playbook named Play1. Play1 is configured to send an email message to a user named User1. You need to modify Play1 to send email messages to a distribution group named Alerts. What should you use to modify Play1?

A. Azure DevOps

B. Azure Application Insights

C. Azure Monitor

D. Azure Logic Apps Designer

Answer: D

QUESTION 112

You create a new Azure subscription.

You need to ensure that you can create custom alert rules in Azure Security Center. Which two actions should you perform? Each correct answer presents part of the solution. NOTE: Each correct selection is worth one point.

A. Onboard Azure Active Directory (Azure AD) Identity Protection.

B. Create an Azure Storage account.

C. Implement Azure Advisor recommendations.

D. Create an Azure Log Analytics workspace.

E. Upgrade the pricing tier of Security Center to Standard.

Answer: BD

QUESTION 113

You need to configure SQLDB1 to meet the data and application requirements.

Which three actions should you recommend be performed in sequence?

A. Mastered

B. Not Mastered

Answer: A

ONLINE RESOURCES

Practice Paper

Link : https://forms.gle/8faDfXxggADzMsKc8

QR Code :

Video Content

Link :

https://www.youtube.com/playlist?list=PLzlh_31VWEFqFBJgQTPNucIO0wVJdjNmS

QR Code :

Chapter 3: Viva Voce Questions

Q 1: What is Azure Security Center?

Answer: Azure Security Center is a unified security management system that strengthens the security posture of your data centers, providing advanced threat protection across your hybrid workloads in the cloud and on-premises.

Q 2: How does Azure manage identity and access?

Answer: Azure uses Azure Active Directory (AD) to manage identity and access, offering features like multi-factor authentication, conditional access, and identity protection to secure access to applications and resources.

Q 3: What is Azure Sentinel?

Answer: Azure Sentinel is a scalable, cloud-native, security information event management (SIEM) and security orchestration automated response (SOAR) solution that provides security analytics and threat intelligence across the enterprise.

Q 4: Describe the role of Azure Firewall.

Answer: Azure Firewall is a managed, cloud-based network security service that protects your Azure Virtual Network resources. It is a stateful firewall as a service with built-in high availability and unrestricted cloud scalability.

Q 5: What are Azure Policies?

Answer: Azure Policies define and enforce rules for your resources, ensuring that your resources stay compliant with your corporate standards and service level agreements.

Q 6: Explain the function of Azure Key Vault.

Answer: Azure Key Vault helps safeguard cryptographic keys and secrets used by cloud applications and services, providing secure access to tokens, passwords, certificates, API keys, and other secrets.

Q 7: What is Azure Information Protection?

Answer: Azure Information Protection (AIP) is a cloud-based solution that helps organizations classify and protect documents and emails by applying labels, which can include encryption, identity, and authorization policies.

Q 8: How does Azure manage data encryption?

Answer: Azure provides data encryption capabilities both at rest and in transit. Azure uses tools like Azure Storage Service Encryption for data at rest and Transport Layer Security (TLS) for data in transit.

Q 9: What are network security groups (NSGs) in Azure?

Answer: NSGs are used to filter network traffic to and from Azure resources in an Azure Virtual Network. An NSG contains security rules that allow or deny inbound or outbound network traffic based on source and destination IP addresses, ports, and protocols.

Q 10: How do you secure data in Azure Storage?

Answer: Security in Azure Storage involves using Azure Active Directory for authentication, role-based access control (RBAC) for authorization, and encryption for data security.

Q 11: What is the Azure Security Benchmark?

Answer: The Azure Security Benchmark provides best practice guidelines for the security configuration of Azure services, helping improve the security of workloads deployed in Azure.

Q 12: How does Azure respond to security incidents?

Answer: Azure has a structured response strategy that includes detection, assessment, diagnosis, stabilization, and closeout, enabling rapid response to security incidents.

Q 13: Explain Azure DDoS Protection.

Answer: Azure DDoS Protection provides enhanced DDoS mitigation features for your applications running in Azure, protecting against DDoS attacks by analyzing traffic and applying mitigation policies.

Q 14: What is Azure Application Gateway?

Answer: Azure Application Gateway is a web traffic load balancer that enables you to manage traffic to your web applications, including SSL termination, cookie-based session affinity, and URL path-based routing.

Q 15: How does Azure VPN Gateway secure communications?

Answer: Azure VPN Gateway is used to send encrypted traffic between an Azure virtual network and an on-premises location over the public internet or to connect Azure virtual networks to each other.

Q 16: What is Azure Multi-Factor Authentication?

Answer: Azure Multi-Factor Authentication is a security measure that requires two or more methods of authentication from independent categories of credentials to verify the user's identity for login or other transactions.

Q 17: How do role-based access controls (RBAC) work in Azure?

Answer: RBAC in Azure provides fine-grained access management for Azure. It allows you to assign permissions to users, groups, and applications at a certain scope.

Q 18: What is the purpose of Azure Blueprints?

Answer: Azure Blueprints simplifies the governance and deployment of resources by creating repeatable sets of Azure resources that enforce organizational standards and requirements.

Q 19: Describe the integration of Azure Security with third-party solutions.

Answer: Azure allows integration with a wide range of third-party security solutions, providing enhanced security capabilities like firewalls, anti-malware, and more, through Azure Marketplace.

Q 20: What are Azure Tags and how do they improve security governance?

Answer: Azure Tags are metadata assigned to Azure resources for resource management, categorization, and governance, aiding in the organization and monitoring of resources for security and compliance.

YouTube Link for Viva Voce Questions:

https://www.youtube.com/playlist?list=PLzlh_31VWEFphGE70F0kXqp7Elh63cpll

QR Code:

YouTube Videos Playlists for all Microsoft Certifications Videos

Microsoft Azure AI Fundamentals AZ-900

Link: https://www.youtube.com/playlist?list=PLzlh_31VWEFq9KU8Gr0ISbfj-TW6k17f8

QR Code:

Microsoft Azure Administrator AZ-104 Microsoft Azure Virtual Desktop AZ-140

Link: https://www.youtube.com/playlist?list=PLzlh_31VWEFq7JHJMuPJZcw-XShaPrUYP

QR Code:

Microsoft Azure Virtual Desktop AZ-140

Link: https://www.youtube.com/playlist?list=PLzlh_31VWEFowmPK_ro41wiljGoGKexGI

QR Code:

Microsoft Azure Developer AZ-204

Link:

https://www.youtube.com/playlist?list=PLzlh_31VWEFqT72UPVCUi6rqRqLBuwMSr

QR Code:

Designing Microsoft Azure Infrastructure Solution AZ-305

Link:

https://www.youtube.com/playlist?list=PLzlh_31VWEFpTerOknh9kgL4eTbhQwDND

QR Code:

Microsoft Azure Devops Engineer AZ-400

Link: https://www.youtube.com/playlist?list=PLzlh_31VWEFpyUIe_DuaeIkcThEfMT_BT

QR Code:

Microsoft Azure Security Engineer AZ-500

Link:

https://www.youtube.com/playlist?list=PLzlh_31VWEFqFBJgQTPNucIO0wVJdjNmS

QR Code:

Microsoft Azure Network Engineer AZ-700

Link:

https://www.youtube.com/playlist?list=PLzlh_31VWEFowujgDl16YDCvsQtmKgEqL

QR Code:

Microsoft Azure Fundamentals AZ-900

Link: https://www.youtube.com/playlist?list=PLzlh_31VWEFpeXZ2p32R1zDsgcbV8kI1K

QR Code:

Microsoft Azure Data Engineer DP-203

Link: https://www.youtube.com/playlist?list=PLzlh_31VWEFp3XTNqoS60UAOzl8NVG-5z

QR Code:

Microsoft Azure Database Administrator DP- 300

Link: https://www.youtube.com/playlist?list=PLzlh_31VWEFpv-rmc2mbpoIqUOqVW_cIo

QR Code:

1. What is the primary purpose of Microsoft Entra ID in Azure security?

A. Store virtual machine disks
B. Manage identities and access
C. Route network traffic
D. Monitor storage performance

Answer: B. Manage identities and access
Reasoning: Microsoft Entra ID is the cloud identity and access management service used to manage users, groups, applications, authentication, and authorization. In AZ-500, identity security is a major topic because attackers often target accounts before infrastructure. Entra ID supports MFA, Conditional Access, identity protection, app registrations, enterprise applications, and privileged access controls. Storage, routing, and performance monitoring are handled by other Azure services. A security engineer must understand Entra ID because secure access is the foundation of Azure security.

2. Which feature should you use to require MFA only when users sign in from risky locations?

A. Azure Policy
B. Conditional Access
C. Network Security Group
D. Resource lock

Answer: B. Conditional Access
Reasoning: Conditional Access applies access decisions based on signals such as user, group, location, device state, application, and sign-in risk. If users sign in from risky or untrusted locations, you can require MFA, block access, or require a compliant device. Azure Policy controls resource compliance, not user sign-in behavior. NSGs filter network traffic, and resource locks prevent deletion or modification. Conditional Access is the correct identity security control for adaptive access enforcement.

3. A company wants administrators to activate privileged roles only when needed. What should be configured?

A. Microsoft Entra Privileged Identity Management
B. Azure Firewall
C. Azure Monitor metrics
D. Storage lifecycle management

Answer: A. Microsoft Entra Privileged Identity Management
Reasoning: Privileged Identity Management, or PIM, provides just-in-time privileged access. Instead of permanently assigning high-privilege roles such as Global Administrator or Owner, users can be made eligible and must activate the role when required. Activation can require MFA, approval, justification, and time limits. This reduces standing privilege and improves security. Azure Firewall protects networks, Azure Monitor tracks telemetry, and lifecycle management manages blob data. For temporary privileged access, PIM is the best solution.

4. Which Azure RBAC role can manage resources but cannot assign access to other users?

A. Owner
B. Contributor
C. Reader
D. User Access Administrator

Answer: B. Contributor
Reasoning: Contributor can create and manage Azure resources but cannot grant access to others. Owner has full access and can assign roles. Reader can view resources only. User Access Administrator can manage access assignments but does not necessarily manage all resources. This distinction is important for least privilege. In AZ-500, you must know that assigning Contributor instead of Owner reduces risk because it prevents privilege delegation.

5. A user needs to read secrets from Azure Key Vault but must not manage the vault. Which permission model should you use?

A. Assign broad subscription Owner access
B. Assign Key Vault Secrets User or equivalent least-privilege role
C. Give the storage account key
D. Assign Network Contributor

Answer: B. Assign Key Vault Secrets User or equivalent least-privilege role
Reasoning: The user only needs to read secrets, so a data-plane Key Vault role such as Key Vault Secrets User is appropriate when using Azure RBAC permission model. This follows least privilege. Subscription Owner is excessive because it grants wide control. Storage account keys are unrelated. Network Contributor manages networking resources and does not grant secret access. Security engineers must distinguish management-plane permissions from data-plane permissions.

6. What is the purpose of a managed identity?

A. Store files in Azure Files
B. Provide an Azure-managed identity for applications to access resources
C. Encrypt disks manually
D. Create DNS records

Answer: B. Provide an Azure-managed identity for applications to access resources
Reasoning: Managed identities allow Azure resources such as VMs, Function Apps, and App Services to authenticate to other Azure services without storing credentials in code. Azure manages the identity lifecycle. For example, an app can use a managed identity to read secrets from Key Vault. This reduces secret leakage risk. It is a key security best practice because hardcoded passwords, client secrets, and connection strings are common attack targets.

7. Which control helps detect leaked credentials and risky sign-ins?

A. Microsoft Entra ID Protection
B. Azure Load Balancer
C. Azure DNS
D. Recovery Services vault

Answer: A. Microsoft Entra ID Protection
Reasoning: Microsoft Entra ID Protection uses risk detections to identify suspicious users and sign-ins, such as leaked credentials, impossible travel, unfamiliar sign-in properties, or risky IP addresses. It can work with Conditional Access to require password changes or MFA. Load Balancer distributes traffic, DNS resolves names, and Recovery Services vault stores backups. For identity risk detection, Entra ID Protection is the correct service.

8. What is the best way to secure access to a production subscription for administrators?

A. Give all admins permanent Owner access
B. Use PIM with eligible roles and approval
C. Share one admin account
D. Disable activity logs

Answer: B. Use PIM with eligible roles and approval
Reasoning: Permanent Owner access creates unnecessary standing privilege. PIM allows eligible role assignments that must be activated only when needed. Activation can require MFA, approval, justification, and limited duration. Shared accounts reduce accountability and should not be used. Disabling logs weakens security monitoring. AZ-500 emphasizes reducing privileged access exposure and maintaining auditability.

9. Which Azure feature allows blocking resource creation in unapproved regions?

A. Azure Policy
B. Microsoft Sentinel
C. Azure Bastion
D. Application Security Group

Answer: A. Azure Policy
Reasoning: Azure Policy can deny deployments that do not meet defined standards, such as allowed locations, allowed VM sizes, required tags, or encryption requirements. If a company permits resources only in specific regions, an allowed locations policy can enforce it. Microsoft Sentinel is for SIEM/SOAR, Bastion is secure VM access, and Application Security Groups help group VMs for NSG rules. Governance enforcement is handled by Azure Policy.

10. A security team wants to prevent accidental deletion of a critical Key Vault. What should be configured?

A. Delete lock
B. Public IP

C. NAT Gateway
D. Blob lifecycle policy

Answer: A. Delete lock
Reasoning: A Delete lock prevents a resource from being deleted even if a user has permissions that would normally allow deletion. This is useful for critical resources such as Key Vaults, production storage accounts, and networking components. A ReadOnly lock would be stricter and block modifications too. Public IP and NAT Gateway are networking resources. Blob lifecycle policies manage data tiering or deletion, not resource protection.

11. What does a Network Security Group do?

A. Encrypt storage automatically
B. Filter inbound and outbound traffic
C. Store secrets
D. Create backups

Answer: B. Filter inbound and outbound traffic
Reasoning: Network Security Groups contain security rules that allow or deny traffic based on source, destination, port, protocol, and direction. NSGs can be associated with subnets or network interfaces. They are fundamental for Azure network security. They do not encrypt storage, store secrets, or create backups. In AZ-500, you must understand NSG rule priority, default rules, service tags, and application security groups.

12. Which service provides centralized network filtering and threat intelligence?

A. Azure Firewall
B. Azure Files
C. Azure Advisor
D. Azure Backup

Answer: A. Azure Firewall
Reasoning: Azure Firewall is a managed cloud network security service. It provides centralized filtering using network rules, application rules, NAT rules, threat intelligence, and logging. It is often deployed in a hub-and-spoke network architecture. NSGs are useful but distributed; Azure Firewall provides centralized control. Azure Files stores file shares, Advisor gives recommendations, and Backup protects data. For central network inspection and control, Azure Firewall is appropriate.

13. You need to securely connect to a VM without exposing RDP or SSH to the internet. What should you use?

A. Azure Bastion
B. Public IP address
C. DNS forwarding
D. Storage SAS token

Answer: A. Azure Bastion
Reasoning: Azure Bastion provides secure RDP and SSH connectivity through the Azure portal or supported clients without requiring a public IP on the VM. It reduces the attack surface by avoiding exposure of ports 3389 and 22 to the internet. A public IP increases exposure. DNS forwarding and SAS tokens are unrelated. For secure VM administration, Bastion is a common AZ-500 answer.

14. Which feature gives Azure PaaS services a private IP address in your virtual network?

A. Private Endpoint
B. Public endpoint
C. Traffic Manager
D. Azure Monitor alert

Answer: A. Private Endpoint
Reasoning: A Private Endpoint maps an Azure PaaS service, such as Storage, SQL Database, or Key Vault, to a private IP address from your VNet. This allows private connectivity and avoids public internet exposure. Private DNS is commonly used with private endpoints so names resolve to private IPs. Traffic Manager provides DNS-based global routing, and Azure Monitor alerts notify on conditions. For private PaaS access, Private Endpoint is correct.

15. What is the key difference between Service Endpoint and Private Endpoint?

A. Service Endpoint gives a private IP; Private Endpoint does not
B. Service Endpoint secures public service access; Private Endpoint uses private IP access
C. Both are identical
D. Private Endpoint is only for virtual machines

Answer: B. Service Endpoint secures public service access; Private Endpoint uses private IP access
Reasoning: Service Endpoints extend VNet identity to supported Azure services and allow restricting access to selected VNets, but the service still uses its public endpoint. Private Endpoint creates a network interface with a private IP in your VNet and connects privately to the service. Private Endpoint usually provides stronger network isolation. This distinction is frequently tested in AZ-500 networking security scenarios.

16. Which feature protects internet-facing web applications from common attacks like SQL injection?

A. Web Application Firewall
B. Azure Backup
C. Azure DNS private zone
D. Recovery Services vault

Answer: A. Web Application Firewall

Reasoning: Web Application Firewall, available with services such as Azure Application Gateway and Azure Front Door, helps protect web applications from common web attacks, including SQL injection and cross-site scripting. It uses managed rule sets and can operate in detection or prevention mode. Backup and Recovery Services vault help restore data but do not block web attacks. DNS private zones provide internal name resolution. WAF is the correct web-layer protection.

17. Which feature should you use to control outbound internet access from private subnets using a static IP?

A. NAT Gateway
B. Azure Bastion
C. Private DNS zone
D. Azure Policy assignment

Answer: A. NAT Gateway
Reasoning: NAT Gateway provides scalable outbound internet connectivity for resources in a subnet. It can use one or more static public IP addresses, giving predictable outbound source IPs. It does not allow inbound internet connections by default, which improves security compared with public IPs on VMs. Bastion provides management access, Private DNS resolves names, and Policy enforces governance. For controlled outbound access, NAT Gateway is the correct service.

18. A company needs to inspect and log traffic between spokes in a hub-and-spoke design. What should be used?

A. Azure Firewall in the hub
B. Local VM firewall only
C. Azure DNS
D. Blob soft delete

Answer: A. Azure Firewall in the hub
Reasoning: In a hub-and-spoke architecture, a central hub network commonly hosts shared services such as Azure Firewall. Spoke traffic can be routed through the hub using user-defined routes, allowing centralized inspection and logging. Local VM firewalls do not provide central visibility. DNS and blob soft delete are unrelated. This design helps enforce consistent security controls across multiple workloads or subscriptions.

19. What is Just-in-Time VM access used for?

A. Permanently opening RDP and SSH ports
B. Temporarily opening management ports only when approved
C. Encrypting VM disks
D. Creating VM snapshots

Answer: B. Temporarily opening management ports only when approved

Reasoning: Just-in-Time VM access, available through Defender for Cloud, reduces exposure by keeping management ports closed until access is requested and approved. Access is granted for a limited time and from limited source IPs. This reduces brute-force and scanning risk. Permanently opening RDP or SSH is unsafe. Disk encryption and snapshots are separate compute protection topics.

20. Which service helps assess Azure security posture and provides secure score recommendations?

A. Microsoft Defender for Cloud
B. Azure DNS
C. Azure Queue Storage
D. Azure Traffic Manager

Answer: A. Microsoft Defender for Cloud
Reasoning: Microsoft Defender for Cloud provides cloud security posture management, recommendations, regulatory compliance views, and secure score. It helps identify misconfigurations, vulnerabilities, and missing protections. It can also provide workload protection plans. DNS, Queue Storage, and Traffic Manager do not assess security posture. AZ-500 includes securing Azure using Defender for Cloud and Microsoft Sentinel as a major domain.

21. Which service should be used for SIEM and SOAR in Azure?

A. Microsoft Sentinel
B. Azure Bastion
C. Azure Files
D. Azure App Service Plan

Answer: A. Microsoft Sentinel
Reasoning: Microsoft Sentinel is Microsoft's cloud-native SIEM and SOAR solution. It collects security data from Azure, Microsoft 365, endpoints, firewalls, and third-party sources. It supports analytics rules, incidents, hunting, workbooks, automation rules, and playbooks. Bastion provides VM access, Azure Files stores file shares, and App Service Plan hosts web apps. For centralized security monitoring and incident response, Sentinel is the right service.

22. What is a Microsoft Sentinel analytics rule used for?

A. Define alert logic based on security data
B. Create a storage account
C. Assign Azure RBAC roles
D. Encrypt a virtual network

Answer: A. Define alert logic based on security data
Reasoning: Analytics rules in Microsoft Sentinel define detection logic that generates alerts and incidents from collected security data. Rules may be scheduled, near-real-time, Microsoft

security, machine learning, or fusion-based. For example, a rule can detect multiple failed sign-ins followed by a successful login. RBAC role assignments, storage account creation, and network encryption are not analytics rule functions.

23. What is a Sentinel playbook commonly used for?

A. Automated response to incidents
B. Increasing VM CPU
C. Creating DNS zones
D. Moving blobs to archive tier

Answer: A. Automated response to incidents
Reasoning: Sentinel playbooks are based on Azure Logic Apps and automate security response actions. For example, a playbook can send a Teams message, create a ticket, disable a user, block an IP, or notify analysts when an incident occurs. This supports SOAR workflows. Scaling VMs, creating DNS zones, and moving blobs are not typical Sentinel playbook purposes.

24. Which query language is used for Microsoft Sentinel hunting and Log Analytics?

A. KQL
B. HTML
C. Bicep
D. YAML only

Answer: A. KQL
Reasoning: Kusto Query Language, or KQL, is used to query logs in Log Analytics and Microsoft Sentinel. Security engineers use KQL for hunting, investigation, dashboards, and analytics rules. HTML is for web pages, Bicep is for infrastructure as code, and YAML is often used for pipelines. AZ-500 candidates should be comfortable reading and understanding KQL queries for security operations.

25. A storage account must reject public network access and allow only private connectivity. What should you configure?

A. Disable public network access and create a Private Endpoint
B. Enable anonymous blob access
C. Add a public IP to the storage account
D. Disable encryption

Answer: A. Disable public network access and create a Private Endpoint
Reasoning: To fully restrict storage access to private connectivity, disable public network access and configure a Private Endpoint. This gives the storage account a private IP within the VNet and prevents access through public endpoints. Anonymous access and public IP exposure are insecure. Encryption should remain enabled. This is a common AZ-500 data protection scenario.

26. Which feature can help recover accidentally deleted blobs?

A. Blob soft delete
B. NAT Gateway
C. Azure Bastion
D. NSG flow logs

Answer: A. Blob soft delete
Reasoning: Blob soft delete protects data from accidental deletion by retaining deleted blobs for a configured period. During that retention period, deleted blobs can be restored. It protects against user or application mistakes, not regional disasters. NAT Gateway provides outbound connectivity, Bastion provides VM access, and NSG flow logs record network traffic metadata. Data recovery features are important in the storage security part of AZ-500.

27. What should you use to protect secrets, keys, and certificates?

A. Azure Key Vault
B. Azure DNS
C. Azure Load Balancer
D. Azure Monitor metrics only

Answer: A. Azure Key Vault
Reasoning: Azure Key Vault is designed to securely store and manage secrets, encryption keys, and certificates. It supports access control, logging, soft delete, purge protection, and integration with managed identities. It prevents secrets from being stored in application code or configuration files. DNS, Load Balancer, and metrics do not protect secrets. Key Vault is central to secure application design in Azure.

28. What is purge protection in Azure Key Vault used for?

A. Prevent permanent deletion during retention period
B. Improve DNS resolution
C. Increase VM CPU performance
D. Route traffic to a firewall

Answer: A. Prevent permanent deletion during retention period
Reasoning: Soft delete allows recovery of deleted Key Vault objects, while purge protection prevents permanent deletion until the retention period expires. This protects against malicious or accidental purging of keys, secrets, or certificates. It is especially important for encryption keys because losing a key may make encrypted data unrecoverable. DNS, CPU performance, and routing are unrelated.

29. Which feature protects Azure SQL Database from suspicious database activities?

A. Microsoft Defender for SQL
B. Azure Bastion
C. Azure DNS private resolver only

D. VM availability set

Answer: A. Microsoft Defender for SQL
Reasoning: Microsoft Defender for SQL provides threat detection and vulnerability assessment for SQL workloads. It can detect suspicious activities such as potential SQL injection, unusual access patterns, or brute-force attempts. Bastion is for VM access, DNS private resolver handles name resolution, and availability sets improve VM availability. Database security in AZ-500 includes protecting SQL, auditing, encryption, and threat detection.

30. Which option helps encrypt Azure Storage data with keys controlled by the customer?

A. Customer-managed keys in Key Vault
B. Public anonymous access
C. Basic SKU public IP
D. Azure DNS

Answer: A. Customer-managed keys in Key Vault
Reasoning: Azure Storage encrypts data at rest by default, but customer-managed keys give organizations greater control over key lifecycle and compliance. The keys are stored in Azure Key Vault or managed HSM, and storage uses them for encryption. Public anonymous access weakens security, and public IP or DNS settings do not control storage encryption. Customer-managed keys are commonly tested in data security scenarios.

31. You need to enforce encryption on all storage accounts automatically. What should you use?

A. Azure Monitor
B. Azure Policy
C. NSG
D. Azure DNS

Answer: B. Azure Policy
Reasoning: Azure Policy allows enforcing compliance rules such as requiring encryption on storage accounts. You can create a policy that audits or denies deployments that do not meet encryption standards. This ensures all resources follow security best practices automatically. Azure Monitor only observes metrics and logs, NSGs control traffic, and DNS resolves names. In AZ-500, governance and compliance enforcement through Policy is a key concept.

32. Which feature allows you to detect brute-force attacks on VMs?

A. Azure Firewall
B. Microsoft Defender for Cloud
C. Azure DNS
D. Azure Backup

Answer: B. Microsoft Defender for Cloud
Reasoning: Defender for Cloud provides threat detection and can identify brute-force attacks against virtual machines by analyzing login patterns. It also provides alerts and recommendations. Azure Firewall filters traffic but does not specifically detect brute-force patterns. DNS and Backup are unrelated. This question tests your understanding of threat detection versus traffic filtering.

33. You need to restrict access to a storage account from specific IP ranges. What should you configure?

A. Storage firewall rules
B. NSG only
C. Azure Monitor alerts
D. Route table

Answer: A. Storage firewall rules
Reasoning: Storage account firewall rules allow restricting access to specific IP addresses or VNets. This is part of network security for data services. NSGs do not apply directly to storage accounts. Route tables control routing, not access. Azure Monitor alerts notify events but do not enforce restrictions.

34. What is the purpose of Microsoft Sentinel data connectors?

A. Encrypt data
B. Ingest data into Sentinel

C. Route traffic
D. Create VMs

Answer: B. Ingest data into Sentinel
Reasoning: Data connectors bring data from sources such as Azure resources, Microsoft 365, firewalls, and third-party systems into Microsoft Sentinel. Without data connectors, Sentinel cannot analyze or detect threats. Encryption and routing are separate concerns. This is a core concept in security operations.

35. You need to monitor suspicious sign-in activity. Which logs should you review?

A. Activity logs
B. Sign-in logs
C. NSG logs
D. Storage logs

Answer: B. Sign-in logs
Reasoning: Sign-in logs in Entra ID provide detailed information about authentication attempts, including location, device, and risk level. Activity logs track resource changes, NSG logs track network traffic, and storage logs track storage access. For identity security, sign-in logs are critical.

36. What is the purpose of Azure DDoS Protection Standard?

A. Encrypt storage
B. Protect against volumetric attacks
C. Monitor logs
D. Manage identities

Answer: B. Protect against volumetric attacks
Reasoning: Azure DDoS Protection Standard provides advanced protection against distributed denial-of-service attacks. It detects and mitigates attacks automatically. It also provides telemetry and integration with Azure Monitor. Encryption, logging, and identity management are handled by other services.

37. You want to allow only secure HTTPS traffic to a web app. What should you configure?

A. NSG rule
B. Application Gateway with HTTPS
C. Azure Backup
D. DNS

Answer: B. Application Gateway with HTTPS
Reasoning: Application Gateway can enforce HTTPS and terminate SSL connections. While NSGs can block ports, Application Gateway provides Layer 7 control and better web security. Backup and DNS are unrelated.

38. What is Azure Defender for Storage used for?

A. Backup storage
B. Threat detection for storage accounts
C. DNS resolution
D. VM scaling

Answer: B. Threat detection for storage accounts
Reasoning: Defender for Storage detects suspicious activities such as unusual access patterns, malware uploads, or data exfiltration attempts. Backup protects data but does not detect threats. DNS and scaling are unrelated.

39. Which feature ensures that deleted Key Vault secrets can be recovered?

A. Soft delete
B. NSG
C. Azure Monitor
D. Route table

Answer: A. Soft delete
Reasoning: Soft delete allows recovery of deleted secrets within a retention period. It prevents accidental loss of critical data. NSG, Monitor, and route tables do not provide recovery.

40. You need to restrict admin access to VMs to specific IPs. What should you use?

A. NSG rules
B. Azure Policy
C. Azure Monitor
D. Storage firewall

Answer: A. NSG rules
Reasoning: NSGs allow filtering traffic based on source IP. You can restrict RDP/SSH access to trusted IP addresses. Policy enforces rules but does not filter traffic.

41. What is the purpose of Just Enough Administration (JEA)?

A. Full admin access
B. Limited admin tasks
C. Network routing
D. Storage encryption

Answer: B. Limited admin tasks
Reasoning: JEA allows users to perform only specific administrative tasks, reducing risk. It follows least privilege principle.

42. Which service provides vulnerability assessment for VMs?

A. Defender for Cloud
B. Azure DNS
C. Azure Backup
D. NSG

Answer: A. Defender for Cloud
Reasoning: Defender for Cloud scans VMs for vulnerabilities and misconfigurations.

43. What is the purpose of Azure Security Benchmark?

A. Pricing model
B. Security best practices
C. Backup policy
D. Network routing

Answer: B. Security best practices
Reasoning: Azure Security Benchmark provides guidelines for securing Azure workloads.

44. You need to log all administrative actions. What should you use?

A. Activity Log
B. NSG logs
C. Storage logs
D. DNS logs

Answer: A. Activity Log
Reasoning: Activity Log tracks control-plane operations like resource creation and deletion.

45. What is Azure Sentinel hunting?

A. Backup process
B. Proactive threat search
C. VM scaling
D. DNS resolution

Answer: B. Proactive threat search
Reasoning: Hunting allows analysts to search for threats using queries.

46. Which feature protects against insider threats?

A. PIM
B. DNS
C. Load Balancer
D. Backup

Answer: A. PIM
Reasoning: PIM reduces risk of misuse by limiting privileged access.

47. What is Azure Confidential Computing?

A. Data encryption during processing
B. Backup
C. DNS
D. Routing

Answer: A. Data encryption during processing
Reasoning: It protects data even while being processed in memory.

48. Which service helps secure APIs?

A. API Management
B. DNS
C. NSG
D. Backup

Answer: A. API Management
Reasoning: It provides authentication, throttling, and monitoring.

49. What is Azure Information Protection?

A. Data classification and protection
B. VM scaling
C. DNS
D. Backup

Answer: A. Data classification and protection
Reasoning: It labels and protects sensitive data.

50. What is role of encryption at rest?

A. Protect stored data
B. Route traffic
C. Monitor logs
D. Manage users

Answer: A. Protect stored data
Reasoning: Encryption at rest ensures data is secure when stored.

51–60 (Condensed but exam-focused reasoning)

51. Secure data in transit → TLS → Protect communication
52. Detect anomalies → Sentinel → SIEM analytics
53. Secure VM access → Bastion → No public IP
54. Prevent deletion → Locks → Resource protection
55. Restrict regions → Policy → Governance
56. Monitor logs → Log Analytics → Query data
57. Secure storage → Private Endpoint → Private access
58. Protect keys → Key Vault → Secure storage
59. Detect threats → Defender → Alerts & insights
60. Automate response → Playbooks → SOAR automation

61. You need to enforce MFA for all users accessing Azure resources. What should you configure?

A. Azure Policy
B. Conditional Access
C. NSG
D. Azure Monitor

Answer: B. Conditional Access
Reasoning: Conditional Access is the primary tool for enforcing MFA in Azure. It allows you to define policies that require MFA based on user, group, location, device compliance, or risk level. While Azure Policy enforces resource configuration, it does not manage identity authentication. NSGs filter network traffic, and Azure Monitor tracks logs and metrics. In AZ-500, identity protection is critical, and enforcing MFA is one of the most important security controls to reduce account compromise risks.

62. Which feature helps identify risky users based on behavior patterns?

A. Azure Monitor
B. Entra ID Protection
C. Azure Firewall
D. Azure Backup

Answer: B. Entra ID Protection
Reasoning: Entra ID Protection uses machine learning to detect suspicious activities such as impossible travel, unfamiliar sign-ins, and leaked credentials. It assigns risk levels to users and sign-ins, which can trigger Conditional Access policies. Azure Monitor focuses on logs and metrics, Firewall filters traffic, and Backup handles data recovery. This feature is crucial for proactive identity security in AZ-500 scenarios.

63. You need to restrict access to Azure resources based on device compliance. What should you use?

A. NSG
B. Conditional Access
C. Azure Policy
D. Route Table

Answer: B. Conditional Access
Reasoning: Conditional Access allows enforcing policies based on device state, such as requiring compliant or domain-joined devices. This ensures only trusted devices can access resources. NSGs and route tables control network traffic, not identity-based conditions. Azure Policy enforces resource configuration, not device compliance.

64. What is the purpose of Azure AD Identity Governance?

A. Manage network traffic
B. Manage identity lifecycle and access reviews
C. Backup data
D. Encrypt storage

Answer: B. Manage identity lifecycle and access reviews
Reasoning: Identity Governance includes features like access reviews, entitlement management, and lifecycle workflows. It ensures users have appropriate access and removes unnecessary permissions over time. This reduces insider threats and privilege creep. It is an important AZ-500 concept.

65. You need to monitor SQL injection attempts on Azure SQL Database. What should you enable?

A. Defender for SQL
B. Azure DNS
C. NSG
D. Backup

Answer: A. Defender for SQL
Reasoning: Defender for SQL detects suspicious activities such as SQL injection attempts and anomalous queries. It provides alerts and recommendations. NSGs cannot detect application-level attacks, and DNS/Backup are unrelated.

66. Which feature provides centralized visibility into security alerts across Azure?

A. Microsoft Sentinel
B. Azure DNS
C. Azure Files
D. Load Balancer

Answer: A. Microsoft Sentinel
Reasoning: Sentinel aggregates security alerts from multiple sources and provides centralized visibility, correlation, and investigation capabilities. It is a SIEM solution.

67. You need to ensure encryption keys are rotated regularly. What should you use?

A. Key Vault with key rotation policy
B. NSG
C. Azure Monitor
D. Route table

Answer: A. Key Vault with key rotation policy
Reasoning: Key Vault supports automatic key rotation policies, ensuring encryption keys are updated periodically. This reduces risk of key compromise.

68. Which feature helps prevent data exfiltration from storage accounts?

A. Private Endpoint
B. Azure DNS
C. Backup
D. Load Balancer

Answer: A. Private Endpoint
Reasoning: Private Endpoint ensures storage access is restricted to private networks, reducing risk of data leakage.

69. What is the purpose of Azure Firewall threat intelligence filtering?

A. Backup data
B. Block known malicious IPs/domains
C. Monitor CPU
D. Create VMs

Answer: B. Block known malicious IPs/domains
Reasoning: Threat intelligence filtering uses Microsoft's threat feed to block traffic from malicious sources automatically.

70. You need to log network traffic for analysis. What should you enable?

A. NSG Flow Logs
B. Azure Policy
C. Backup
D. DNS

Answer: A. NSG Flow Logs
Reasoning: NSG Flow Logs capture metadata about network traffic, useful for security analysis and troubleshooting.

71. Which Azure service provides endpoint protection for VMs?

A. Defender for Servers
B. Azure DNS
C. Backup
D. Load Balancer

Answer: A. Defender for Servers
Reasoning: Defender for Servers provides threat detection, vulnerability assessment, and endpoint protection.

72. You need to restrict access to Key Vault based on network location. What should you configure?

A. Firewall rules
B. NSG
C. Backup
D. DNS

Answer: A. Firewall rules
Reasoning: Key Vault firewall allows restricting access to specific IPs or VNets.

73. What is Azure Sentinel workbooks used for?

A. Visualization dashboards
B. Backup
C. DNS
D. Routing

Answer: A. Visualization dashboards
Reasoning: Workbooks provide interactive dashboards for analyzing security data.

74. You need to enforce encryption for VMs. What should you use?

A. Disk Encryption
B. NSG
C. DNS
D. Backup

Answer: A. Disk Encryption
Reasoning: Azure Disk Encryption protects VM disks using encryption technologies.

75. What is purpose of Azure Security Center recommendations?

A. Improve security posture
B. Backup
C. DNS
D. Routing

Answer: A. Improve security posture
Reasoning: Recommendations guide users to fix vulnerabilities and improve security.

76–90 (Condensed but high-value reasoning)

76. Detect anomalies → Sentinel → Correlate alerts
77. Secure API → API Management → Authentication + throttling
78. Secure VM → JIT → Temporary access
79. Protect data → Encryption → Confidentiality
80. Secure identity → MFA → Prevent breaches

81. Monitor logs → Log Analytics → Query data
82. Protect secrets → Key Vault → Central storage
83. Secure network → Firewall → Central filtering
84. Prevent attacks → WAF → Web protection
85. Control access → RBAC → Least privilege
86. Secure storage → Private Endpoint → No public exposure
87. Detect threats → Defender → Alerts
88. Automate response → Playbooks → SOAR
89. Monitor compliance → Policy → Governance
90. Protect keys → HSM → Hardware security

91. You need to block access to Azure resources from countries with high risk. What should you configure?

A. NSG rules
B. Conditional Access with location-based policy
C. Azure Policy
D. Route table

Answer: B. Conditional Access with location-based policy
Reasoning: Conditional Access allows enforcing access rules based on geographic location. You can block or require MFA for users signing in from high-risk countries. NSGs filter IP traffic but do not understand user identity or geographic risk. Azure Policy enforces resource compliance, not user access. Route tables control traffic paths. Identity-based access control is the correct approach for location-based restrictions.

92. A security team wants alerts when suspicious activities occur across multiple Azure services. What should they use?

A. Azure Monitor metrics
B. Microsoft Sentinel
C. NSG
D. Azure DNS

Answer: B. Microsoft Sentinel
Reasoning: Microsoft Sentinel is a SIEM solution that aggregates logs and alerts from multiple sources. It uses analytics rules to detect suspicious activities and generate incidents. Azure Monitor collects data but does not provide full SIEM capabilities. NSGs and DNS are unrelated. Sentinel is designed for centralized security monitoring and incident response.

93. You need to ensure that only compliant devices can access Azure resources. What should you use?

A. Azure Policy
B. Conditional Access with device compliance
C. NSG
D. Backup

Answer: B. Conditional Access with device compliance
Reasoning: Conditional Access can enforce access rules based on device compliance status. Devices must meet security requirements such as encryption and antivirus before access is granted. Azure Policy enforces resource configuration, not device compliance.

94. Which feature helps protect against credential theft attacks?

A. MFA
B. NSG

C. Azure DNS
D. Backup

Answer: A. MFA
Reasoning: Multi-Factor Authentication adds an additional verification step beyond passwords, making credential theft less effective. Even if passwords are compromised, attackers cannot access accounts without the second factor.

95. You need to monitor failed login attempts across Azure. What should you use?

A. Sign-in logs
B. NSG logs
C. Backup logs
D. DNS logs

Answer: A. Sign-in logs
Reasoning: Sign-in logs provide details about authentication attempts, including failures, locations, and risk levels. This helps detect brute-force attacks.

96. Which feature provides automated threat response in Azure?

A. Sentinel playbooks
B. NSG
C. DNS
D. Backup

Answer: A. Sentinel playbooks
Reasoning: Playbooks automate responses to security incidents, such as blocking IPs or notifying admins. They are part of SOAR capabilities.

97. You need to secure communication between Azure services without exposing them publicly. What should you use?

A. Private Endpoint
B. Public IP
C. DNS
D. Load Balancer

Answer: A. Private Endpoint
Reasoning: Private Endpoint ensures traffic stays within Azure network, eliminating exposure to public internet.

98. Which feature helps detect malware in storage accounts?

A. Defender for Storage
B. NSG

C. DNS
D. Backup

Answer: A. Defender for Storage
Reasoning: Defender for Storage scans uploads and detects malware or suspicious activity.

99. You need to enforce encryption for all disks. What should you use?

A. Azure Policy
B. NSG
C. DNS
D. Backup

Answer: A. Azure Policy
Reasoning: Policy can enforce disk encryption compliance across all VMs.

100. Which feature provides hardware-based key protection?

A. Azure Managed HSM
B. Key Vault basic
C. NSG
D. Backup

Answer: A. Azure Managed HSM
Reasoning: Managed HSM provides hardware-level security for cryptographic keys.

101. You need to secure web applications globally. What should you use?

A. Azure Front Door with WAF
B. NSG
C. DNS
D. Backup

Answer: A. Azure Front Door with WAF
Reasoning: Front Door provides global routing and WAF protection.

102. Which feature helps detect insider threats?

A. PIM
B. DNS
C. Backup
D. Load Balancer

Answer: A. PIM
Reasoning: PIM limits privileged access and monitors usage, reducing insider risk.

103. You need to log all changes to Azure resources. What should you use?

A. Activity Log
B. NSG logs
C. DNS logs
D. Backup logs

Answer: A. Activity Log
Reasoning: Activity Log records all control-plane operations.

104. Which feature helps classify sensitive data?

A. Azure Information Protection
B. NSG
C. DNS
D. Backup

Answer: A. Azure Information Protection
Reasoning: It labels and protects sensitive data.

105. You need to secure container images. What should you use?

A. Defender for Containers
B. NSG
C. DNS
D. Backup

Answer: A. Defender for Containers
Reasoning: It scans images for vulnerabilities.

106. Which feature helps prevent data exfiltration?

A. Private Endpoint
B. DNS
C. Backup
D. Load Balancer

Answer: A. Private Endpoint
Reasoning: Restricts data access to private network only.

107. You need to monitor network connectivity issues. What should you use?

A. Network Watcher
B. NSG
C. DNS
D. Backup

Answer: A. Network Watcher
Reasoning: Provides troubleshooting tools for network issues.

108. Which feature helps automate security tasks?

A. Azure Automation
B. NSG
C. DNS
D. Backup

Answer: A. Azure Automation
Reasoning: Automates repetitive security operations.

109. You need to restrict VM access to specific users. What should you use?

A. RBAC
B. NSG
C. DNS
D. Backup

Answer: A. RBAC
Reasoning: RBAC controls who can access resources.

110. Which feature helps detect unusual network patterns?

A. NSG Flow Logs
B. DNS
C. Backup
D. Load Balancer

Answer: A. NSG Flow Logs
Reasoning: Provides network traffic insights.

111–120 (Condensed Expert Reasoning)

111. Secure identity → Conditional Access → Policy enforcement
112. Detect threats → Sentinel → SIEM analytics
113. Protect data → Encryption → Confidentiality
114. Secure APIs → API Management → Control access
115. Monitor logs → Log Analytics → Query data
116. Protect secrets → Key Vault → Secure storage
117. Secure network → Firewall → Central filtering
118. Prevent attacks → WAF → Web protection
119. Control access → RBAC → Least privilege
120. Automate response → Playbooks → SOAR

121. You need to ensure that Azure resources comply with security standards continuously. What should you use?

A. Azure Monitor
B. Azure Policy
C. NSG
D. Azure DNS

Answer: B. Azure Policy
Reasoning: Azure Policy continuously evaluates resources for compliance and can enforce rules such as encryption, allowed locations, and tagging. It can audit existing resources and deny non-compliant deployments. Azure Monitor collects logs but does not enforce compliance. NSGs control traffic, and DNS resolves names. For governance and compliance enforcement, Azure Policy is essential in AZ-500 scenarios.

122. Which feature helps detect suspicious activity in Azure SQL Database?

A. Defender for SQL
B. NSG
C. DNS
D. Backup

Answer: A. Defender for SQL
Reasoning: Defender for SQL provides advanced threat detection, identifying anomalies such as SQL injection attempts, unusual login patterns, or data exfiltration. It generates alerts and recommendations. NSGs filter traffic but do not analyze database queries. DNS and Backup are unrelated. This question tests knowledge of workload-specific protection in AZ-500.

123. You need to enforce encryption in transit for all web applications. What should you configure?

A. HTTPS-only setting
B. NSG
C. Azure Policy
D. Route table

Answer: A. HTTPS-only setting
Reasoning: Enabling HTTPS-only ensures all traffic between clients and web applications is encrypted using TLS. This protects data from interception. NSGs cannot enforce encryption, and Policy may audit but not directly enforce HTTPS behavior at runtime. Encryption in transit is a core security principle.

124. Which service helps centralize logs from multiple Azure resources?

A. Log Analytics Workspace
B. NSG

C. DNS
D. Backup

Answer: A. Log Analytics Workspace
Reasoning: Log Analytics Workspace collects and stores logs from various Azure resources. It allows querying using KQL and supports monitoring, troubleshooting, and security analysis. NSGs and DNS do not centralize logs. Backup stores data but not logs.

125. You need to automate response to security incidents. What should you use?

A. Sentinel playbooks
B. NSG
C. DNS
D. Backup

Answer: A. Sentinel playbooks
Reasoning: Sentinel playbooks automate incident response actions such as sending alerts, blocking IPs, or creating tickets. They are part of SOAR capabilities. NSGs and DNS do not automate responses.

126. Which feature helps detect vulnerabilities in container images?

A. Defender for Containers
B. NSG
C. DNS
D. Backup

Answer: A. Defender for Containers
Reasoning: Defender for Containers scans container images for vulnerabilities and misconfigurations, helping secure container workloads.

127. You need to restrict access to Azure resources based on user risk level. What should you use?

A. Conditional Access with risk-based policies
B. NSG
C. Azure Policy
D. Backup

Answer: A. Conditional Access with risk-based policies
Reasoning: Conditional Access integrates with Entra ID Protection to enforce policies based on user or sign-in risk levels. This allows blocking or requiring MFA for risky users.

128. Which feature helps secure secrets used in applications?

A. Azure Key Vault

B. NSG
C. DNS
D. Backup

Answer: A. Azure Key Vault
Reasoning: Key Vault securely stores and manages secrets, keys, and certificates, preventing exposure in code.

129. You need to monitor network traffic patterns for anomalies. What should you use?

A. NSG Flow Logs
B. DNS
C. Backup
D. Load Balancer

Answer: A. NSG Flow Logs
Reasoning: NSG Flow Logs provide detailed information about network traffic, helping detect unusual patterns.

130. Which feature helps enforce least privilege access?

A. RBAC
B. NSG
C. DNS
D. Backup

Answer: A. RBAC
Reasoning: RBAC ensures users only have permissions necessary for their tasks, reducing security risks.

131. You need to secure web applications against OWASP attacks. What should you use?

A. WAF
B. NSG
C. DNS
D. Backup

Answer: A. WAF
Reasoning: Web Application Firewall protects against common web vulnerabilities like SQL injection and XSS.

132. Which feature helps prevent unauthorized VM access?

A. Just-in-Time access
B. NSG
C. DNS

D. Backup

Answer: A. Just-in-Time access
Reasoning: JIT limits VM access by opening ports only when needed and for limited time.

133. You need to encrypt sensitive data in storage. What should you use?

A. Encryption at rest
B. NSG
C. DNS
D. Backup

Answer: A. Encryption at rest
Reasoning: Encryption at rest ensures stored data is protected from unauthorized access.

134. Which feature helps monitor compliance status?

A. Azure Policy compliance dashboard
B. NSG
C. DNS
D. Backup

Answer: A. Azure Policy compliance dashboard
Reasoning: It provides visibility into compliance across resources.

135. You need to secure hybrid connectivity. What should you use?

A. VPN Gateway or ExpressRoute
B. NSG
C. DNS
D. Backup

Answer: A. VPN Gateway or ExpressRoute
Reasoning: These services provide secure connectivity between on-prem and Azure.

136. Which feature helps classify and protect sensitive documents?

A. Azure Information Protection
B. NSG
C. DNS
D. Backup

Answer: A. Azure Information Protection
Reasoning: It labels and protects sensitive data.

137. You need to detect anomalies in user behavior. What should you use?

A. Entra ID Protection
B. NSG
C. DNS
D. Backup

Answer: A. Entra ID Protection
Reasoning: It analyzes user behavior to detect suspicious activities.

138. Which feature helps secure API access?

A. API Management
B. NSG
C. DNS
D. Backup

Answer: A. API Management
Reasoning: It provides authentication, throttling, and monitoring.

139. You need to ensure data integrity during transmission. What should you use?

A. TLS encryption
B. NSG
C. DNS
D. Backup

Answer: A. TLS encryption
Reasoning: TLS ensures secure and tamper-proof communication.

140. Which feature helps automate patch management?

A. Update Management
B. NSG
C. DNS
D. Backup

Answer: A. Update Management
Reasoning: It automates OS patching for VMs.

141–150 (Condensed Expert-Level Reasoning)

141. Detect threats → Defender → Alerts & recommendations
142. Secure storage → Private Endpoint → No public access
143. Monitor logs → Log Analytics → Query data
144. Secure identity → MFA → Strong authentication
145. Prevent deletion → Resource Lock → Protection

146. Secure keys → Managed HSM → Hardware security
147. Control traffic → Firewall → Central filtering
148. Protect web apps → WAF → OWASP protection
149. Enforce governance → Policy → Compliance rules
150. Automate security → Playbooks → SOAR workflows

151. You need to ensure that only approved applications can access Azure resources. What should you use?

A. Conditional Access with app-based conditions
B. NSG
C. Azure Policy
D. Route table

Answer: A. Conditional Access with app-based conditions
Reasoning: Conditional Access allows restricting access based on specific applications. You can allow or block access depending on the app being used, ensuring only approved apps interact with Azure resources. NSGs and route tables manage network traffic, while Azure Policy governs resource configuration. This question tests identity-based access control.

152. Which feature helps detect anomalous resource usage patterns?

A. Azure Monitor with alerts
B. NSG
C. DNS
D. Backup

Answer: A. Azure Monitor with alerts
Reasoning: Azure Monitor collects metrics and logs and can trigger alerts when unusual patterns occur, such as spikes in CPU or network usage. This helps detect potential attacks or misconfigurations. NSGs and DNS do not analyze usage patterns.

153. You need to protect sensitive data during processing. What should you use?

A. Azure Confidential Computing
B. NSG
C. DNS
D. Backup

Answer: A. Azure Confidential Computing
Reasoning: Confidential Computing protects data while it is being processed in memory using secure enclaves. This ensures data is protected even from administrators.

154. Which feature helps secure Kubernetes clusters?

A. Defender for Containers
B. NSG
C. DNS
D. Backup

Answer: A. Defender for Containers

Reasoning: Defender for Containers provides security monitoring, vulnerability assessment, and threat detection for AKS clusters.

155. You need to enforce password reset for high-risk users. What should you use?

A. Conditional Access with risk policy
B. NSG
C. Azure Policy
D. Backup

Answer: A. Conditional Access with risk policy
Reasoning: Conditional Access can require password reset when user risk is high, improving account security.

156. Which feature helps monitor API usage and detect abuse?

A. API Management analytics
B. NSG
C. DNS
D. Backup

Answer: A. API Management analytics
Reasoning: API Management provides analytics, throttling, and monitoring to detect abnormal API usage.

157. You need to secure communication between VNets. What should you use?

A. VNet Peering with encryption
B. NSG
C. DNS
D. Backup

Answer: A. VNet Peering with encryption
Reasoning: VNet Peering allows secure, private communication between VNets using Azure backbone.

158. Which feature helps detect malware in virtual machines?

A. Defender for Servers
B. NSG
C. DNS
D. Backup

Answer: A. Defender for Servers
Reasoning: Defender for Servers provides endpoint protection and malware detection.

159. You need to restrict access to storage based on user identity. What should you use?

A. RBAC
B. NSG
C. DNS
D. Backup

Answer: A. RBAC
Reasoning: RBAC controls access to storage resources based on identity.

160. Which feature helps automate security compliance checks?

A. Azure Policy
B. NSG
C. DNS
D. Backup

Answer: A. Azure Policy
Reasoning: Azure Policy continuously evaluates compliance and enforces rules.

161. You need to secure web apps from bot attacks. What should you use?

A. WAF with bot protection
B. NSG
C. DNS
D. Backup

Answer: A. WAF with bot protection
Reasoning: WAF includes bot protection rules to block automated malicious traffic.

162. Which feature helps detect insider threats in Azure?

A. PIM and audit logs
B. DNS
C. Backup
D. Load Balancer

Answer: A. PIM and audit logs
Reasoning: PIM reduces privilege misuse and audit logs track actions.

163. You need to ensure secure key storage with hardware protection. What should you use?

A. Managed HSM
B. Key Vault basic
C. NSG
D. Backup

Answer: A. Managed HSM
Reasoning: Managed HSM provides hardware-based key protection.

164. Which feature helps detect suspicious network traffic?

A. NSG Flow Logs
B. DNS
C. Backup
D. Load Balancer

Answer: A. NSG Flow Logs
Reasoning: NSG Flow Logs provide insights into traffic patterns.

165. You need to secure data pipelines. What should you use?

A. Encryption and RBAC
B. NSG
C. DNS
D. Backup

Answer: A. Encryption and RBAC
Reasoning: Secure pipelines require encryption and controlled access.

166. Which feature helps monitor compliance with regulations?

A. Compliance dashboard
B. NSG
C. DNS
D. Backup

Answer: A. Compliance dashboard
Reasoning: Provides visibility into regulatory compliance.

167. You need to secure hybrid identity. What should you use?

A. Azure AD Connect
B. NSG
C. DNS
D. Backup

Answer: A. Azure AD Connect
Reasoning: Synchronizes on-prem identity with Azure.

168. Which feature helps detect phishing attacks?

A. Defender for Office 365
B. NSG
C. DNS
D. Backup

Answer: A. Defender for Office 365
Reasoning: Detects phishing and email threats.

169. You need to restrict admin actions based on approval. What should you use?

A. PIM approval workflow
B. NSG
C. DNS
D. Backup

Answer: A. PIM approval workflow
Reasoning: Requires approval before privileged role activation.

170. Which feature helps secure data analytics workloads?

A. Azure Purview
B. NSG
C. DNS
D. Backup

Answer: A. Azure Purview
Reasoning: Provides data governance and classification.

171–180 (Condensed Expert Reasoning)

171. Detect anomalies → Monitor → Alerts
172. Secure storage → Private Endpoint → Isolation
173. Protect identity → MFA → Strong auth
174. Monitor threats → Sentinel → SIEM
175. Secure keys → Key Vault → Protection
176. Control access → RBAC → Least privilege
177. Protect network → Firewall → Filtering
178. Secure apps → WAF → Web protection
179. Enforce rules → Policy → Compliance
180. Automate response → Playbooks → SOAR

181. You need to prevent users from creating public IP addresses in a subscription. What should you use?

A. NSG
B. Azure Policy (deny public IP creation)
C. Azure Monitor
D. Route Table

Answer: B. Azure Policy (deny public IP creation)
Reasoning: Azure Policy can enforce governance by denying the creation of public IP resources. This helps reduce exposure of resources to the internet. NSGs can restrict traffic but cannot prevent resource creation. Azure Monitor tracks metrics, and route tables control traffic routing. For compliance and governance enforcement, Azure Policy is the correct solution.

182. Which feature helps detect lateral movement attacks inside a network?

A. Defender for Cloud (network insights)
B. DNS
C. Backup
D. Load Balancer

Answer: A. Defender for Cloud (network insights)
Reasoning: Defender for Cloud analyzes network activity and can detect suspicious lateral movement between resources. It uses analytics and threat intelligence to identify abnormal communication patterns.

183. You need to enforce that all resources must use private endpoints. What should you configure?

A. Azure Policy
B. NSG
C. DNS
D. Backup

Answer: A. Azure Policy
Reasoning: Azure Policy can enforce the use of private endpoints by denying resources that do not meet this requirement. This ensures all services are accessed privately.

184. Which feature helps protect against zero-day vulnerabilities?

A. Defender for Cloud
B. NSG
C. DNS
D. Backup

Answer: A. Defender for Cloud

Reasoning: Defender for Cloud uses threat intelligence and behavioral analytics to detect unknown threats, including zero-day attacks.

185. You need to monitor unusual API calls across Azure. What should you use?

A. Activity Log + Sentinel
B. NSG
C. DNS
D. Backup

Answer: A. Activity Log + Sentinel
Reasoning: Activity Logs track API calls, and Sentinel analyzes them for suspicious patterns.

186. Which feature helps enforce secure configurations for Kubernetes?

A. Azure Policy for AKS
B. NSG
C. DNS
D. Backup

Answer: A. Azure Policy for AKS
Reasoning: Azure Policy integrates with AKS to enforce security standards such as restricting privileged containers.

187. You need to restrict access to a VM based on time of day. What should you use?

A. Conditional Access
B. NSG
C. DNS
D. Backup

Answer: A. Conditional Access
Reasoning: Conditional Access can enforce time-based access restrictions for users.

188. Which feature helps secure secrets in DevOps pipelines?

A. Key Vault integration
B. NSG
C. DNS
D. Backup

Answer: A. Key Vault integration
Reasoning: Key Vault securely stores secrets and integrates with pipelines.

189. You need to monitor compliance violations in real-time. What should you use?

A. Azure Policy + alerts
B. NSG
C. DNS
D. Backup

Answer: A. Azure Policy + alerts
Reasoning: Policy evaluates compliance continuously and can trigger alerts.

190. Which feature helps detect data exfiltration attempts?

A. Defender for Storage
B. NSG
C. DNS
D. Backup

Answer: A. Defender for Storage
Reasoning: It detects unusual data access patterns and potential exfiltration.

191. You need to secure communication between microservices. What should you use?

A. TLS + Private networking
B. NSG
C. DNS
D. Backup

Answer: A. TLS + Private networking
Reasoning: Encryption and private connectivity ensure secure service communication.

192. Which feature helps detect compromised accounts?

A. Entra ID Protection
B. NSG
C. DNS
D. Backup

Answer: A. Entra ID Protection
Reasoning: It identifies risky users and sign-ins.

193. You need to ensure secure VM boot process. What should you use?

A. Trusted Launch
B. NSG
C. DNS
D. Backup

Answer: A. Trusted Launch

Reasoning: Trusted Launch protects against boot-level attacks.

194. Which feature helps enforce encryption for databases?

A. Transparent Data Encryption
B. NSG
C. DNS
D. Backup

Answer: A. Transparent Data Encryption
Reasoning: TDE encrypts database files at rest.

195. You need to secure web traffic globally. What should you use?

A. Front Door + WAF
B. NSG
C. DNS
D. Backup

Answer: A. Front Door + WAF
Reasoning: Provides global routing and web protection.

196. Which feature helps detect unauthorized changes?

A. Activity Log alerts
B. NSG
C. DNS
D. Backup

Answer: A. Activity Log alerts
Reasoning: Alerts notify when changes occur.

197. You need to secure identity federation. What should you use?

A. Entra ID federation
B. NSG
C. DNS
D. Backup

Answer: A. Entra ID federation
Reasoning: Allows secure identity integration.

198. Which feature helps monitor insider threats?

A. Audit logs + PIM
B. DNS

C. Backup
D. Load Balancer

Answer: A. Audit logs + PIM
Reasoning: Tracks and limits privileged actions.

199. You need to secure IoT devices in Azure. What should you use?

A. Defender for IoT
B. NSG
C. DNS
D. Backup

Answer: A. Defender for IoT
Reasoning: Provides threat detection for IoT environments.

200. Which feature helps enforce security baselines?

A. Azure Security Benchmark
B. NSG
C. DNS
D. Backup

Answer: A. Azure Security Benchmark
Reasoning: Provides recommended security practices.

201–210 (Condensed Expert-Level Reasoning)

201. Detect threats → Sentinel → SIEM analytics
202. Secure identity → MFA → Prevent breaches
203. Protect data → Encryption → Confidentiality
204. Secure APIs → API Management → Control access
205. Monitor logs → Log Analytics → Insights
206. Protect secrets → Key Vault → Secure storage
207. Secure network → Firewall → Filtering
208. Prevent attacks → WAF → Web protection
209. Enforce governance → Policy → Compliance
210. Automate response → Playbooks → SOAR

211. A company wants to ensure that no secrets are hardcoded in application code. What should they implement?

A. Azure Key Vault with managed identities
B. NSG
C. Azure DNS
D. Backup

Answer: A. Azure Key Vault with managed identities
Reasoning: Hardcoding secrets is a major security risk. Azure Key Vault allows secure storage and retrieval of secrets, while managed identities enable applications to authenticate without storing credentials. This eliminates secret exposure in code. NSGs control traffic, DNS resolves names, and Backup protects data but does not manage secrets. This is a common AZ-500 best practice question.

212. You need to detect unusual spikes in outbound data transfer. What should you use?

A. Azure Monitor + alerts
B. NSG
C. DNS
D. Backup

Answer: A. Azure Monitor + alerts
Reasoning: Azure Monitor tracks metrics like network throughput and can trigger alerts for abnormal spikes. This helps detect potential data exfiltration. NSGs filter traffic but do not analyze patterns. DNS and Backup are unrelated. Monitoring abnormal behavior is critical for threat detection.

213. Which feature helps protect against privilege escalation attacks?

A. PIM
B. DNS
C. Backup
D. Load Balancer

Answer: A. PIM
Reasoning: Privileged Identity Management reduces risk of privilege escalation by limiting access duration and requiring approval. It ensures no user has permanent high privileges.

214. You need to secure communication between on-premises and Azure. What should you use?

A. VPN Gateway or ExpressRoute
B. NSG
C. DNS
D. Backup

Answer: A. VPN Gateway or ExpressRoute
Reasoning: These services provide secure connectivity between on-premises and Azure, with encryption and private routing.

215. Which feature helps detect compromised virtual machines?

A. Defender for Servers
B. NSG
C. DNS
D. Backup

Answer: A. Defender for Servers
Reasoning: It provides threat detection, vulnerability assessment, and endpoint protection.

216. You need to ensure that only encrypted connections are allowed to storage accounts. What should you configure?

A. Secure transfer required
B. NSG
C. DNS
D. Backup

Answer: A. Secure transfer required
Reasoning: This setting forces HTTPS connections, ensuring encryption in transit.

217. Which feature helps enforce data residency requirements?

A. Azure Policy (location restrictions)
B. NSG
C. DNS
D. Backup

Answer: A. Azure Policy (location restrictions)
Reasoning: Policy can restrict resource deployment to specific regions.

218. You need to monitor suspicious login attempts in real-time. What should you use?

A. Entra ID Protection + alerts
B. NSG
C. DNS
D. Backup

Answer: A. Entra ID Protection + alerts
Reasoning: Provides real-time risk detection and alerting.

219. Which feature helps protect against DDoS attacks?

A. Azure DDoS Protection Standard
B. NSG
C. DNS
D. Backup

Answer: A. Azure DDoS Protection Standard
Reasoning: It detects and mitigates large-scale attacks automatically.

220. You need to secure Azure SQL Database connections. What should you use?

A. Private Endpoint + firewall rules
B. NSG
C. DNS
D. Backup

Answer: A. Private Endpoint + firewall rules
Reasoning: Ensures secure and restricted access.

221. Which feature helps detect suspicious API activity?

A. Sentinel analytics rules
B. NSG
C. DNS
D. Backup

Answer: A. Sentinel analytics rules
Reasoning: Detect abnormal API usage patterns.

222. You need to secure container registries. What should you use?

A. Defender for Containers
B. NSG
C. DNS
D. Backup

Answer: A. Defender for Containers
Reasoning: Scans images for vulnerabilities.

223. Which feature helps enforce password policies?

A. Entra ID settings
B. NSG
C. DNS
D. Backup

Answer: A. Entra ID settings
Reasoning: Controls password complexity and expiration.

224. You need to secure communication between services using certificates. What should you use?

A. Key Vault certificates
B. NSG
C. DNS
D. Backup

Answer: A. Key Vault certificates
Reasoning: Provides secure certificate management.

225. Which feature helps detect abnormal network flows?

A. NSG Flow Logs + analytics
B. DNS
C. Backup
D. Load Balancer

Answer: A. NSG Flow Logs + analytics
Reasoning: Provides insights into unusual traffic patterns.

226. You need to ensure secure DevOps pipelines. What should you use?

A. Key Vault + RBAC
B. NSG
C. DNS
D. Backup

Answer: A. Key Vault + RBAC
Reasoning: Secure secrets and restrict access.

227. Which feature helps automate compliance remediation?

A. Azure Policy with remediation tasks
B. NSG
C. DNS

D. Backup

Answer: A. Azure Policy with remediation tasks
Reasoning: Automatically fixes non-compliant resources.

228. You need to secure sensitive logs. What should you use?

A. Encryption + RBAC
B. NSG
C. DNS
D. Backup

Answer: A. Encryption + RBAC
Reasoning: Protect logs from unauthorized access.

229. Which feature helps detect insider misuse of privileges?

A. PIM audit logs
B. DNS
C. Backup
D. Load Balancer

Answer: A. PIM audit logs
Reasoning: Tracks privileged actions.

230. You need to secure serverless applications. What should you use?

A. Managed identities + Key Vault
B. NSG
C. DNS
D. Backup

Answer: A. Managed identities + Key Vault
Reasoning: Avoid storing secrets and secure access.

231–240 (Condensed Ultra-Advanced Reasoning)

231. Detect threats → Sentinel → SIEM correlation
232. Secure identity → Conditional Access → Adaptive security
233. Protect data → Encryption → Confidentiality
234. Secure APIs → API Management → Gateway control
235. Monitor logs → Log Analytics → Deep insights
236. Protect secrets → Key Vault → Central storage
237. Secure network → Firewall → Central inspection
238. Prevent attacks → WAF → Web defense
239. Enforce compliance → Policy → Governance

240. Automate response → Playbooks → SOAR